# COMPLETE HUMANITY IN JESUS

# COMPLETE HUMANITY IN JESUS

## A Theological Memoir

JOHN M. KEITH

NEWSOUTH BOOKS
Montgomery | Louisville

NewSouth Books
105 South Court Street
Montgomery, AL 36104


Copyright © 2009 by John M. Keith.
All rights reserved under International and Pan-American Copyright Conventions.
Published in the United States by NewSouth, Inc.,
Montgomery, Alabama.

Library of Congress Cataloging-in-Publication Data available by request.

ISBN-13: 978-1-60306-047-9
ISBN-10: 1-60306-047-2

Photograph on page 5 and back cover author photograph by Lauren C. K. Goslin.
The illustration on page 12 was drawn by Jeffrey Slaton, after the author's sketch.

Design by Randall Williams

Printed in the United States of America

FOR LENNOX AND ARABELLA

# CONTENTS

# Introduction

*"The glory of God is humanity fully alive"* — IRENAEUS[1]

The journey of faith involves a quest for true and full humanity, both an understanding of what it means to be perfectly
human and a way of becoming human. For Christians this
journey causes a perennial enigma: Jesus is for us the revelation of
perfect, complete, true, full humanity; but the perfect, complete, true,
full humanity of Jesus can be recognized only as we become human
and become aware of the partial and emerging humanity we see in
ourselves and in others.

What follows in the chapters of this book reflects on the dialectic
between recognizing humanity in ourselves and others, then seeing it
perfectly modeled in Jesus, and recognizing the perfection of humanity in Jesus, then seeing it partially and often distortedly reflected in
ourselves and others. Sometimes the movement is more dominant
from the delight of discovering humanity in ourselves and in the world
around us, which leads us to see its perfection in Jesus. At other times
the movement is initially from recognizing the full and true humanity of Jesus, which brings us to the sad recognition of the failed and
unrealized aspects of our humanity. But the dialectical movement is
always both ways, back and forth, like taking steps with the right foot
and the left foot on a lifelong journey of faith.

The Church began to think about the human nature of Christ in
a philosophically systematic way in the fifth century in response to
controversies in which some perspectives were deemed to be hereti-
cal. These dialogues were summarized in two principle statements,

---

1   Quoted by Thomas J. Long, "Living by the Word," p. 19, *The Christian Century,*
    March 21, 2006, vol. 123, no. 6

which express the orthodox position: the Definition of Chalcedon from the Council of A.D. 451, which was originally written in Greek, and the (so-called) Athanasian Creed, which scholars today believe was originally written in Latin in an era later than the lifetime of St. Athanasius, probably in Gaul.[2]

The particular details of the controversies, heresies, and theological terms and fine points of the late fourth and fifth century debates are beyond the scope of this meditation. In no way is it intended, however, to argue with or modify those ancient orthodox formulas. Although the emphasis of the meditation here will be on the human nature of Christ, there is no intention to deny or compromise the divine nature of Christ. In focusing on the human nature of Christ it may be difficult to avoid the implication of failing to recognize the "two natures, without division, without separation."[3] Perhaps in later meditations we may reflect on the divine nature of Christ and on the union of the two natures of Christ. It is the premise of this meditation, however, that the human nature of Christ must be the beginning place for an understanding of our humanity as well as the beginning place for our understanding of God.

The perspective here is different from Anselm's *Cur Deus Homo* in its rather exclusive emphasis on God becoming man only in order to be sacrificed. The Incarnation in this meditation reflects more broadly on God becoming man in order to reveal and restore true, complete, perfect, full humanity, in which the sacrifice on Calvary was a major factor.

From the Definition of Chalcedon and the Creed of St. Athanasius it may be instructive to look at the meaning of a few of the Greek and Latin words and phrases before beginning the meditation, which is based on a wide personal selection of ad hoc examples in religion,

2  "The Athanasian Creed," pp. 98-99, *The Oxford Dictionary of the Christian Church,* F. L. Cross, editor, Oxford University Press, London,1958

3  "Definition of the Union of the Divine and Human Natures in the Person of Christ" and "Quicunque Vult commonly called The Creed of St. Athanasius," pp. 864-865, *The Book of Common Prayer,* The Episcopal Church, The Church Hymnal Corporation and the Seabury Press, New York, 1977

history, culture, nature, theology, philosophy, and psychology.

The relevant part of the Athansian Creed reads, "Thus the right faith is that we believe and confess that our Lord Jesus Christ, the Son of God, is both God and man *(Deus et homo est)*. As God, He was begotten of the Father before time; as man, He was born in time of the substance of His Mother *(et homo est ex substantia matris in saeculo natus)*. He is perfect God; and He is perfect man, with a rational soul and human flesh *(Perfectus Deus, perfectus homo: ex anima rationali et humana carne subsistens)* . . . and He is one, not because His divinity was changed into flesh, but because His humanity was assumed unto God *(sed assumptione humanitatis in Deum)*. He is one, not by a mingling of substances, but by unity of person *(sed unitate personae)*. As a rational soul and flesh are one man: so God and man are one Christ *(Nam sicut anima rationalis et caro unus est homo: ita Deus et homo unus est Christus)."*[4]

From the Definition of Chalcedon, the relevant words and phrases for our purpose are " . . . our Lord Jesus Christ, at once complete in Godhead and complete in manhood, truly God and truly man consisting also of a reasonable soul and body *(teleion ton auton en Thetati, teleion ton auton en anthropotati, Theon alethos kai antropon alethos, ton auton ek psyches logikes kai somatos)*; of one substance *(homoousios)* with the Father as regards his Godhead, and at the same time of one substance *(homoousios)* with us as regards his manhood; like us in all respects apart from sin."[5]

The reflection that follows often employs the adjectives "perfect" *(perfectus)* from the Athanasian Creed and "complete" *(teleion)*, sometimes also interpreted to mean fully, made perfect, completed, and perfect; and "truly" *(alethos)* sometimes expressed as true, full, real, genuine, from the Definition of Chalcedon.

The examples of ways by which we discover our humanity are drawn

---

4  Latin and translation from "Quicumque Athanasian Creed" www.creeds.net/ancient/Quincumque

5  Greek and translation from William Bright, *The Canons of the First Four General Councils,* second edition, Oxford University Press, 1892, pp. xxxiii-xxxvi

from my personal experience and observation and are described in four rather arbitrarily selected categories: self, other people, human history, and Nature.

A visualization of these four quadrants is approximated in the following diagram:

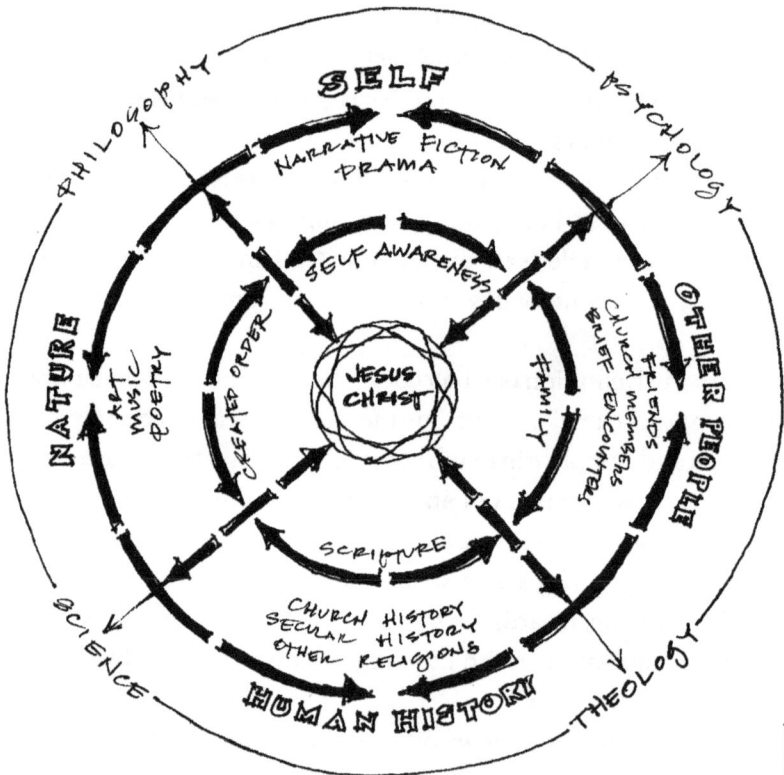

PHILOSOPHY — SELF — PSYCHOLOGY

NARRATIVE FICTION
DRAMA

SELF AWARENESS

NATURE

ART
MUSIC
POETRY

CREATED ORDER

JESUS CHRIST

FAMILY

FRIENDS
CHURCH MEMBERS
BRIEF ENCOUNTERS
STRANGERS

OTHER PEOPLE

SCRIPTURE

CHURCH HISTORY
SECULAR HISTORY
OTHER RELIGIONS

SCIENCE

HUMAN HISTORY

THEOLOGY

Jeff Slaton

It is possible to begin at any point in one of the circles surrounding "Jesus Christ," but the Christian journey of faith always involves the dialectic between that point and Jesus. The circles might be imagined to move like a kaleidoscope, at times abutting each other from different positions. Their positions may also "jump" to another location: the reading of scripture in *lectio divina* manner, for instance, may initiate inner self-awareness. The lines between positions may also blur and dissolve: for example, self-understanding can hardly develop apart from encounters with other people. Outer circles may also replace the inner circles around Jesus Christ as people mature: while the family would probably involve the first encounters with other people, the church or friendships might offer the primary locus for revelatory encounters with other people later in life. Interpretive methodologies are represented by a "floating circle" outside the contiguous positions in the diagram. Philosophy, psychology, theology, and science do not usually offer immediate revelations of what it means to be human but rather give us a rational structure for interpreting those revelations. Once again, however, the diagram should not be regarded too rigidly or too literally. On occasions even the technical categories of philosophy or psychology or theology or science may elicit a moment of insight into what it means to be truly human.

My intention had been to include a few italicized biographical anecdotes that corresponded to the expository text at the bottom of every third or fourth page, somewhat like pictorial illustrations. Alas, the more I wrote about one anecdote the more others occurred to me and grew like kudzu across a Georgia hillside until they finally overwhelmed the book and almost choked the life out of it. I have attached them to the end of each section, sometimes rivaling or even surpassing the length of the original chapters. I hope that they may still be evocative and illustrative of the themes without too much distraction. They are set down not chronologically but as they seem to resonate with the subjects taken up in the expositions which precede them. I would suggest that they be read, if they are read at all, where they are placed after you finish with each chapter before moving on to the next section.

With all of those caveats let us begin arbitrarily and personally with the quadrant of "other people." I am not so arrogant as to assume that the examples and anecdotes from my life are in any way definitive or even typical for other people, but it is my hope that they may evoke the personal memories and reflections of those who read ahead.

# Finding Our Humanity
# As We Encounter Other People

*"Christ Jesus . . . emptied himself, taking the form of a slave, being born in human likeness."* — PHILIPPIANS 2: 7 (NRSV)

The first hint of what it means to be human may come when we gaze into our parents' faces as infants. Some extraordinary people may be able to recall that moment. I could not. The moment may be recapitulated, however, when we hold our newborn children and witness their eyes searching for the pattern of our faces. The delight of seeing my baby daughter searching my face as I searched hers was rivaled only by holding my newborn grandchildren decades later.

For most people parents are the first point of reference in their search for the meaning of their humanity. In two of the four Gospel accounts we meet Mary and Joseph, as well as other kinfolk and ancestors, before we are introduced to Jesus. Perhaps one of the reasons that Jesus did not marry and father children was to let us know that having a spouse and begetting a child are not necessary for becoming fully human. Yet, Jesus did take children into his arms in the way a parent holds a baby.[1] Jesus himself as an infant was taken into the arms of the elderly Simeon who praised God upon looking into his face as also did the eighty-four-year-old prophetess, Anna.[2]

---

1  Matthew 19: 13-15; Mark 10: 15-16; Luke 18: 15-17. Only Luke designates them as "infants" (*brepos*); Matthew and Mark refer to them as "young children" (*paidon*).

2  Luke 2: 25-38

Jesus's relationship with his parents became more complicated as he grew older and began to understand more fully the complexities of his humanity and theirs. When he was twelve years old, Jesus questioned why his parents could not understand him, as countless numbers of adolescents have asked over the centuries.[3] Later in his life the lack of understanding of his vocation by his mother and siblings grew even deeper.[4]

Jesus taught both the necessity of leaving parents and kin[5] but also affirmed the requirement to honor parents.[6] On the Cross Jesus still expressed concern and sought care for his mother.[7] Most people navigate this ambiguity in our relationships with our parents, when we search for the meaning of our humanity as we grow older.

My first introduction to Jesus was from hearing "Jesus loves me, this I know . . . ." sung to me and seeing pictures and pageants and crèches of baby Jesus in the manger. For many years my mother played the piano in the church nursery and taught toddlers to sing "Jesus loves me . . . ." with her. My earliest memory of her and of Jesus was her singing that cradle hymn to me and then with me. Long before I encountered Jesus in the scriptures of the Gospels he had become familiar in music and art, and that mediation would be important in my Christian journey throughout my life.

The certainty that I was loved was conveyed by parents as well as by grandparents and aunts and uncles and cousins from the days of my infancy. My mother's only sister, many years younger, seemed to understand me better than anyone else. Aunt Dot's gifts at Christmas and on my birthday were the most desirable and thrilling things I received. She intuited my interests and fears, my wants and needs. When I was hospitalized for eye surgery as a very young child, she alone was able to distract me. Dot lost her beloved first husband to cancer soon after

---

3   Luke 2: 41-51
4   Matthew 12: 46-50; Mark 3: 31-35; Luke 8: 19-21
5   Matthew 19: 29; Mark 10: 29; Luke 14: 26 and 18:29
6   Matthew 19: 19; Mark 10: 19; Luke 18: 20
7   John 19: 25-27

they were married. That's when her drinking started, although alcoholism also afflicted others in my mother's family, her father and several of her brothers (and explained Mother's abhorrence of alcohol and her absolute teetotalism). Even as a child I overheard laments about Aunt Dot's drinking and occasional bizarre sexual debauchery when she was drunk. As an adult I witnessed the deterioration and destruction, both emotional and physical, of that beautiful woman whom I loved dearly and who loved me just as dearly. It is possible to discern the outlines of complete humanity not only in its partial manifestations but also in the shape of the cavities left when it has been eaten away and lost. Jesus' loving nature was my first understanding of his humanity; and when I discovered the flaws and inadequacies in the love of other people, even parents and close family members, the perfection of human love in Christ became more urgently sought.

My father's pride in a first-born son, his namesake, was diminished when it became evident that I would not be the athlete he had longed for. Eye muscles weak from birth resulting in surgeries before I was two years old and lifelong double vision meant that the gift of a football from an older cousin would never enjoy much use. Eventually my father took pride in some of my artistic and academic achievements, but the yearning to be loved as I was and the desire to accept others without measuring out my love in proportion to their utility and attractiveness impelled the search for a purer love in the full humanity of Jesus.

Some events in Jesus' life have been almost eerily replicated in my life. A painting in the Kindergarten Sunday School room of my childhood Baptist Church became an early visual image of Jesus. My Sunday School teacher said it portrayed Jesus as a little boy in the Temple in Jerusalem. I later learned it was intended to portray the child Samuel before Eli, but for me it will always represent the boyhood of Jesus. The incident of the twelve year old Jesus seperated from his parents in the Temple was recalled when I stayed after school to help with a drama club project painting stage sets. Although I was probably older than twelve, I had not yet gotten my driver's license; and my mother became frantic when I did not arrive home on the school bus. My negligence in calling her was more than matched by her anxious tirade. Later it became apparent that my mother was suffering from a mental illness that required a hospitalization for treatment. The lingering effects of her mental problems and then early onset of Alzheimer's disease opened my eyes to damaged and diminished humanity which longs for healing and restoration in Christ. Sometimes we see humanity in its realized goodness in other people. Especially as we become aware of our parents' feet of clay, we look for the fullness of humanity in the absent spaces of their lives.

After discovering marks of humanity in various people—friends, colleagues, siblings, spouses, children and grandchildren, church members—we may later in life return to survey our parents and understand their humanity more deeply and more sympathetically. As I saw more and more of my father's traits in myself, I became more forgiving of his flaws and more appreciative of his steadfast concern and loyal perseverance. After many years I was able to get behind the decades of my mother's mental and emotional problems to reclaim memories of her kind grace and charming warmth. The love between Jesus and his mother was perhaps most fully and deeply evident as he was dying. If Mary had questioned Jesus' vocation out of fear for his safety earlier, she later prayed with his followers and his brothers.[8]

The discovery of aspects of humanity in our siblings can be another leg on our journey of faith. My childhood relationship with my brother and sister may not be universal, but it would seem to be typical. Rivalry and quarreling characterized our activities more than appreciation of each others' real humanity. My brother and I were engaged in a perennial spat, and we teased my sister unmercifully about being fat—she was actually, if anything, normally and handsomely plump compared to her brothers' scrawny thinness.

We have only scant references to Jesus' siblings during his earthly ministry and none from childhood. Besides the encounter with them and his mother early in his ministry, John comments in an aside

---

8  John 19:25-27; Acts 1: 14

that "not even his brothers believed in him."[9] It may be that Jesus' most complex family conflict was with his cousin, John the Baptist, a relationship that may never have been completely resolved at least in this world upon earth. The request of the Risen Christ that Mary Magdalene go and tell his brothers about his appearance probably refers to his disciples, although later at least some of his family played important roles in the early church, especially his brother James, who was its most prominent leader.[10]

There were moments in my early years when I was forced to recognize aspects of humanity through events involving my siblings, usually from the negative outlines of guilt and remorse. When I pushed my brother off the front porch and he had to be taken to the hospital to sew up the gashes in his leg, I experienced a rush of concern and fear for his well-being even greater than the dread of my parents' punishment. My sister's tears often brought at least momentary guilt and regret.

We do not know how Jesus and his siblings might have interacted in the physical world as older adults after his early thirties. As noted, siblings did come to a new evaluation and appreciation of him after his resurrection.

My brother and sister and I became good and close friends in our more mature years. As with parents, we tend to return to other family members as our years increase. For my brother and me our sister is our greatest defender and advocate. My brother and I can count on each others' support and loyalty. When we contemplated traveling to Peru together in our sixties (although one of us was only approaching 60), we wondered if the rivalries and quarrels of our childhood would resurface in that isolated context without the mediation of other family members or the focus on our children; but our relationships had been transformed into adult friendships.

The role of spouses is the most difficult relationship to fit into our model of the journey of faith seeking full humanity because Jesus did not marry or have conjugal relations, except in the most fanciful

9   John 7: 5
10  Galatians 1: 19

fictional accounts. Jesus did affirm the state of matrimony both in his teachings and in his presence and blessing at a wedding,[11] and one of the most frequent metaphors for heaven in his parables was the marriage feast. Yet, psycho-sexual development and coital experience challenge and may distract from the search for true humanity. My own delayed and protracted psycho-sexual development and my first experience of coition later in life than most men so often obsessed my thoughts and emotions that I was deflected from a focus on the meaning of being human. Erotic desire, even when it is mutually fulfilling and gener-ously considerate of the other, hardly distinguishes human nature from the natural animal unless it is transfigured by self-sacrificing love (*agape*). Nevertheless, the union of spouses serves as a metaphor for divine-human union in scripture. In the Hebrew scriptures Yahweh is described as being like a husband to Israel and in the New Testament the Church is called the bride of Christ.[12] Yet, unlike the Muslim belief, in orthodox Christian faith Jesus never married or engaged in coital behavior. As noted above, we can speculate that Jesus never married or had offspring in order to affirm that these conditions are not necessary for attaining complete humanity.

Most people, however, will seek their humanity as they work through their sexual and marital experiences. As is the case with parents and siblings and children, the quest for humanity will be developed as these relationships are transformed into friendship. The struggle to become and remain and develop as friends for a husband and wife is the most challenging human relationship because of their constant proximity in space and the lifelong duration of their time together.

For Rilla and me the shared responsibility of parenthood was the beginning of true friendship. Our shared interests and endeavors and aspirations drew us together during courtship and into the early years of marriage and beyond; but rivalry, jealousy, and selfishness always threatened and compromised our mutual support. Marriage may be

---

11  Matthew 19; 4-6; Mark 10: 6-9; John 2: 1f
12  See the imagery in Hosea 2: 16 and Revelation chapters 21 and 22, especially Revelation 22: 17

described as a lifelong process of lovers becoming best friends. Because it is both lifelong and inescapably constant, the highest expressions of friendship and the greatest threats and perils and deficiencies of friendship may be manifested in a marriage. Parenthood brings a special urgency to the need for married partners to become friends. That Jesus offers us no explicit example makes the obligation even more difficult. In its very difficulty as well as in its necessity, however, searching for and partially fulfilling our true humanity as spouses (and later as parents) become all the more compelling.

Although Jesus never had biological progeny, the relationship of parent and child is not as far removed from us in him as is that of husband and wife, because Jesus was a son and nurtured children. Even so, those of us who rear children undergo a process over many years that has no exact correlation in the example of Jesus' earthly life.

We were blessed and cursed with a headstrong, willful daughter. Almost from the time Lauren could crawl across the room she wanted to go her way on her own terms. The other side of her personality was a caring, cuddling child who seemed preternaturally sensitive to other people's feelings and ever valiant in defending people or animals that had been mistreated or abused. Watching her stumble, succeed, and sometimes fail in her search for her own humanity forced me to examine more closely the parameters of my humanity. The greatest lesson that children can teach, however, may be that their ultimate destiny cannot be controlled and hence their humanity and my humanity are not subject to my control. The waiting period for our children to grow into adults is a long and often agonizing stretch of time. After the passing of decades, however, the possibility may open for us to have an adult friendship together. Then, as with our relationships with parents and siblings and spouses which have been transformed into adult friendships, the full dimensions of the boundaries of what it means to be human can be mutually explored in ourselves and in them as we encounter them and they encounter us.

We may recognize how our children have become adults through many events, but among the most common and poignant are those that involve witnessing our children as parents. Grandchildren elicit all the feelings and memories of our own children's infancy and youth. Lennox and Arabella directly inspire joy and hope and also bring renewed joy and hope as I witness developing aspects of humanity in their parents, especially my daughter. I am forced by my grandchildren to recall the flaws in my humanity that became evident in my role as father but also to exult in the ways my humanity emerged and was enlarged in parenthood. As our children begin to assume even some responsibilities for parenting us, their parents, we see new facets of humanity in ourselves and in them. Looking at the beginning of a human life on earth toward the end of a human life on earth affords a vision of the possibilities of true and full humanity.

Jesus taught that spouses and brothers and sisters, as well as parents and children, may be left behind in the journey of faith;[13] and it was in the context of the spiritual community with disciples and among friends where the fullness of what it means to be human was revealed most clearly during his earthly ministry. Even today friendship and relationships in the church, the spiritual community of his continuing body and presence in the world, may be the most immediate crucibles for the discovery of the fullness of humanity. Parents and siblings and spouses, indeed even our own children, must become our mature friends before their role as the mutual expositors of our humanity develops.

Friendship for our considerations here covers a broad swath of relationships: people connected to us through emotional ties or common interests, mentors and disciples, teachers and students, church members, masters and servants or slaves (to use biblical terminology), and even those encountered briefly and intensely and rarely or never seen again. In the Gospel narratives most of Jesus' relationships would fit one of these types of "friendship"; and friends may often be the most significant "others" in our journey of faith, especially if we consider

---

13 Matthew 19: 29; Mark 10: 29; Luke 18: 29. Only Luke includes spouses among those who may be left behind. That Matthew and Mark do not include spouses may signify that this relationship is more enduring, even in the face of conflicting faith.

how family members may with maturity become friends.

The continuity of the Gospel narrative relies on the relationship between Jesus and his disciples. The role of master, mentor, teacher varied in emphasis depending on the time and occasion. Teacher (rabbi) was perhaps the vocational role that people of his own time usually associated with Jesus during his earthly ministry. The mentors and teachers who have shaped and directed the path of my journey of faith are so numerous that they cannot all be recounted here. From grade school through high school, college, and seminary, as well as from church groups, teachers have influenced my every major decision: what I considered as a life vocation, where I would attend college and seminary, what books I would read and interests I would pursue, where I would live and work, how I would expend my energies, to what I would devote my passionate efforts. Space allows for only a scant few to be named: Lola Bozeman first exposed me to good literature; Anne Montgomery Reid not only nurtured my early passion for music but also helped me connect it to Christian faith and the Church, counteracting adolescent rebellion; Mary Elder planted the notion of matriculating at Duke University rather than a closer-by state school; William Blackburn taught me to write decent prose; Grady Jarrard and Bill Smith nudged me toward the ministry and seminary; Sam Hill supported my attending Harvard Divinity School rather than a denominational seminary; I. B. Holley, Robert Durden, William Hamilton, C. Conrad Wright, Harold Parker, Georges Florovsky, George Earnest Wright, and Frank Moore Cross taught me to think historically, as Paul Tillich, Reinhold and R. R. Niebuhr, Krister Stendahl, and Helmut Koester taught me to think theologically; and Sam Miller, Lawrence Burckholder, Ernst Klein, Warren Carr, Julius Corpening, Edward Haynsworth, Bill Stough, and (again) Grady Jarrard taught me to think and behave pastorally. Beneath and behind the decisions and specific insights nourished by the relationships reflected in each of these names, questions and doubts and aspects of identity and meaning were unearthed and shared and wrestled with. Yet, in each of those mentors and teachers, there were flaws and inadequacies and even occasional betrayals. In their good and gracious gifts to my life, I formed a vision of a true master, mentor, teacher; and from their failings I imagined the outline of the full humanity of a complete and perfect master, mentor, teacher.

The short time frame of three years or less described in the Gospel accounts does not allow us to see, except between the lines, the detailed personalities of those who would later lead the Church and whose memories would shape the faith of future centuries and whose martyrdoms would inspire generations and centuries of Christians. Even more important for revealing the essence of humanity than the models of master, mentor, teacher in my life, however, was the perspective from the opposite direction as I saw both the possibility and the incompleteness of a fully realized humanity in my adolescent quarrelsomeness as well as devotion (like that of John and James, sons of Zebedee), and in my questioning doubts as well as belief (like Thomas) and in my obtuseness as well as insight (like Philip) and in my betrayals (like Judas) and above all in my denials as well as faithfulness (like Peter).

When roles are reversed, seams often appear in the fabric of our lives that permit the light revealing the meaning of humanity to shine through. As I became older, I assumed the role of mentor from time to time. In my early ministry I was still looking up to mentors a decade or more older than I was for guidance and finding young people as much as a decade younger than I was looking to me. Mission trips to the Cherokee Indian reservation in North Carolina and to Central America and outreach projects aiding people in poverty opened the eyes and hearts of young people with new insights into the diverse expressions and varied manifestations of the human spirit, and I was able both to guide and interpret their insight and to benefit from seeing people afresh through their experiences. Their quest for the meaning of what it means to be human not only recalled the earlier stages of my own journey but also gave me a different perspective besides my own experience.

The teachers in the Temple in Jerusalem were amazed and probably delighted by their conversation with the twelve year old Jesus.[14] Jesus was later saddened by the rich young man who was unable to relinquish his love of wealth and security to accompany him on a journey of faith.[15] As in all our relationships with other people the disappointments and failings of those we love also demonstrate from the negative side, through the outline of the vacant space, some of the dimensions of true humanity.[16]

The conversation between Jesus and the rich young man was one of many brief encounters in the Gospel narrative. The Syro-Phoenician woman, the centurion, the woman who touched the fringe of his shawl among many healings, the Samaritan woman at Jacob's well, Nicodemus, Jairus, Zacchaeus, the widow placing her mite in the Temple treasury, various Pharisees, Sadducees, scribes, and publicans are only examples of Jesus' brief encounters. Each of them reveals some aspect of what it means to be truly human. Our lives are also studded with thousands of brief encounters every year that illuminate some aspect of humanity if we but open our eyes and our spirits to their message.

Especially in Luke's Gospel we find encounters with Jesus by those who would usually be excluded because of their race or class or nationality or gender or profession, and many lessons from these encounters are reinforced by parables. Samaritans and tax collectors (publicans) and adulterers are immediately recognized as outsiders, but other people who received Jesus' personal attention and affection are less obvious. When Mary received instruction rather than helping Martha in the kitchen, we usually focus on the contrasts in the two sisters' priorities; but for a woman to receive such attention from a rabbi was almost revolutionary.[17] Children were usually ignored and marginalized in the society of the first century Middle East, but Jesus explicitly asked that children be brought to him.[18]

---

14 Luke 2: 46-47
15 Matthew 19: 16-23; Mark 10: 17-23; Luke 18: 18-24
16 See Mark 10: 21
17 Luke 10: 38-41
18 Matthew 19: 35-15; Mark 10: 13-16; Luke 18: 15-17

Zacchaeus was excluded from polite society like many other publicans because he was a tax collector, but he had two other reasons for being discriminated against: he was short, and he was rich.[19] Although Jesus condemned unmerited wealth like his prophetic predecessors in the Old Testament almost more than any other subject, he was willing to accept Zacchaeus as a wealthy individual person in warm and embracing intimacy. We can observe the same dissonance between his teaching and behavior with regard to adulterous women.

Often there seems to be a conflict between Jesus' teaching and his behavior regarding those who were excluded. Especially regarding foreigners Jesus taught his disciples to minister first to "the lost sheep of the house of Israel"[20] (although he also spoke about "sheep that are not of this fold").[21] Yet, in his own ministry, Jesus often healed and welcomed those of other, often despised races and nationalities and professions. We can speculate that some of the instructions to his disciples may have merely echoed the prejudices of his time as a pedagogical device to open in a deliberate way their consciousness for inclusion by his actions. In any case, Jesus' predilection for including outsiders was a hallmark of his behavior and created the possibility of the inclusion of Gentiles in God's plan of salvation through the Church (as we shall explore in a later section).

In my own experience and observation of being excluded and then included in a social setting or being inclined toward excluding other people and repenting of that impulse so as to include them have been among the most potent moments for discovering my humanity. Attaining a predisposition for inclusion of the outsider and the excluded may be one of the most important presuppositions in finding the nature of true humanity.

Some of the most notable (because noticed) brief encounters in my life happened on mission trips abroad, especially those involving a team of young people. The strangeness of different cultures and customs

19 Luke 19: 2-10
20 Matthew 10: 6
21 John 10: 16

may encourage us more readily to see human elements that stand out from the background, as perhaps happened for Jesus' disciples who witnessed his encounters with centurions and Syro-Phoenicians and Samaritans. Not only did I experience a glimpse of humanity from people who showed kindness and generosity and patience, despite their poverty and unjust, disadvantaged conditions; but I was also able to look at them through the fresh, untutored eyes of young people for whom they seemed as strange and alien as creatures from another planet. The almost shocking expressions of generosity and hospitality illustrated for us an understanding of generosity and hospitality as cardinal marks of humanity.

By contrast a category of encounters may be found in those friend-ships outside our family circles which endure over years and decades. No clear record exists of such enduring relationships in Jesus' life. In fact, he was spurned by the people of his hometown when he returned for a visit; and they even threatened him.[22] Perhaps the nearest equiva-lent of enduring friendship for Jesus was exhibited in the women who followed him from Galilee and remained faithful, keeping watch at the Cross.[23] In my own life a group of friends that I met in grade school or even earlier have kept up with me. They stayed mostly near my home-town all of their lives while I traveled to another state for college and to New England for seminary and to Latin America and Europe for work and study. I would have lost track of them, but they kept in touch with me. Their qualities of faithfulness and loyalty can only be viewed from the vantage of succeeding decades of time, and faithfulness and loyalty are foundational elements of true humanity.

In my entire life there have been no more than a half dozen soul friends or intimate kindred spirits, with whom I could share my deepest and sometimes darkest secrets and explore my most profound doubts and reveal my most humiliating insecurities and fears. There are hints, although not explicit narratives, that Jesus enjoyed such an intimate relationship with his cousin, John the Baptist; but only John, son of

22  Matthew 13: 54-58; Mark 6: 1-6; Luke 4: 16-30
23  Matthew 27: 55; Mark 15: 41; Luke 23: 49

Zebedee, the apostle and evangelist, is referred to as the disciple that Jesus (especially) loved.[24]

In this inclusive category of friendship the words of Christ in the fifteenth chapter of John are especially poignant: "I do not call you servants *(doulos)* any longer, because the servant does not know what the master *(kyrios)* is doing; but I have called you friends *(philos)* . . . ."[25]

Because Jesus so often mentioned the relationship of master and servant in his parables as well as in his brief encounters, we must consider its implications for us in a changed cultural and social context. In the religious tradition of Jesus' heritage the faithful believer was often referred to as a servant of God.[26] Although Jesus was addressed as Master or Lord *(kyrios)* more than with any other title, he taught explicitly and in numerous parables that true humanity requires a reversal of roles, so that the master becomes servant to the servant. Especially by washing his disciples feet, Jesus left the supreme example of the servanthood of lordship.[27]

In my very young childhood there were servants in our home, the wives and younger children of our black tenant families. During those years I was too young to understand the meaning of servanthood beyond recognizing the care and kindness of adults other than my family members. Even before true adolescence I began to sense there was something very wrong about the institution of servanthood as it was practiced in the rural southern United States in the early twentieth century, although by that time due to dramatic economic changes both in our family and in the wider Southern society, few black servants remained in our or other middle class homes; but some guilt from those early years must have touched my emerging consciousness that impelled me to become deeply involved in the civil rights movement during my early adulthood.

---

24 John 19: 26

25 John 15: 15

26 See for instance reference to Abraham in Psalm 105: 32, a motif we shall need to explore more fully in a later section.

27 John 13: 14-15

Still, I did not understand Jesus' teachings and example about servanthood until my years working with the Church in Nicaragua. Once again I was thrust into an environment where the master-servant relationship was an integral aspect of the social and cultural milieu. In Central America during the latter half of the twentieth century, perhaps not unlike the southern United States during the first half of the twentieth century, we could not have functioned very easily without the labor and care of people serving in our homes. The same kind of care and loyalty from servants could be experienced in both worlds; but in my emerging maturity and humanity and in an environment that encouraged greater dignity and respect, we could more readily reverse our roles, so that with Emmalina and Carlos and Tana and Martín I could sometimes become their servant and offer care and healing and nurture and encourage their independence and autonomy and dignity.

Our parish in Nicaragua was composed of wealthy nationals and expatriates, including several ambassadors, and poor members who worked as domestics in homes and in lowly positions in hotels and restaurants. More than at any other place or time in my life I witnessed as well as experienced people humbling themselves in the context of the church, where masters served servants and recognized their dignity and humanity.

The Apostle Paul more profoundly influenced the Christian understanding of the person of Christ than any other believer who did not witness the fleshly incarnation of Jesus, and his theology of Jesus' human nature is summarized in a "kenotic" hymn in the letter to the church in Philippi.[28] This "kenosis" or emptying of divine preeminence in order to take the form of a servant or slave as a human being was the redemptive expression of humility which culminated in his obedience even to dying on a cross. It should be noted in Paul's letters, as well as in the Gospels that the Greek word *doulos* is sometimes translated "slave" and sometimes "servant"; but there is usually no distinction in the New Testament, even within the context of the passage, between

---

28 Philippians 2: 5-11

servants and slaves. The exaltation of the Risen Christ is based upon this emptying of divine prerogative into human form and Jesus' obedience to see his incarnation through to the end in painful and humiliating death. For Paul the supreme expression of Jesus' humanity (and perhaps also most revealing clue to his divinity in his humanity) were as servant and slave.

It would not seem possible, at least from my own experience as well as from the biblical accounts, to be aware of one of the important facets of full humanity from the teachings and example of Jesus without the opportunity to reverse one's position of authority and become a servant to those who would ordinarily serve us according to the normative strata of the secular world.

When servants live close to us in our homes, they may become surrogate families, but I have enjoyed other surrogate families as Jesus also did. From the time I left my parents' home for college and then in seminary and especially during the early years of my ministry before I was married, families took me into the intimate circle of their homes and made me a surrogate son and sibling. The Hams and McCullers in Durham, North Carolina, Ollie Kitchens and the Shockleys in Heflin, Alabama, the Rinns, the Skinners, the Pfeiffers, the Currins, and the Stephens in Managua, Nicaragua, all became like family for me. Over the years I shared the weal and woe of their lives, as they shared the high points and low valleys of my life. Even when I moved away from their vicinities, I would return for visits and always have a welcomed place and familiar bed in their homes. Surrogate families have a certain advantage over consanguinal families, because they are not as preoccupied by the dynamics of control and possessiveness nor by the threats of scandal or prejudicial identification. Thus the transition to adult friendship is more naturally accomplished.

Such a place for Jesus was the home of Mary and Martha and Lazarus in the suburb of Bethany a short walk from the center of Jerusalem. We all need a refuge from the trials and stresses of our work, where we can relax and be ourselves without assuming professional roles. The death of "his friend" Lazarus was one of the few recorded instances of Jesus' weeping.[29] Jesus retreated to Bethany during Holy Week and lodged at least some of those days with Mary and Martha and Lazarus, his surrogate family and home of refuge when he was in Jerusalem.[30]

All of my surrogate families have been in the homes of church members. Besides the relationships of mentor-teacher-master and disciple-student-servant, the church community affords many other encounters with people that open possibilities for discovering our humanity. Every kind of relationship is found within the church from kin even to enemy. The distinction between relationships in the church and those in the secular world are not found in any categorical differences but rather from the context in which they occur. Members of the church share allegiance to Jesus and presumably some common values, morals, and aspirations. Disagreements about the interpretation of those presumably shared values, morals, and aspirations, however, may result in greater conflict and debate than emerge from encounters in the secular world. It is that very debate and conflict which force us to ponder the meaning of our humanity more deeply.

It was not with atheists nor with adherents of other religions nor with Roman authorities that Jesus debated and experienced conflict but with the most devout of his own tradition (the Pharisees) and with the institutional leaders of his theocracy (the Saducees and priests) and with the teachers of adherents of his religion (the scribes). Socially and politically these were most nearly his equals. As those most emotionally and intimately close to us, the members of our families, cause us to ponder certain aspects of our humanity, so those who are our social equals, especially fellow members of the church, create situations where we ruminate on the boundaries of our humanity. When conflict and debate cross the line of civility and respect so that an equal becomes an enemy, the limits of humanity are especially challenged. Although the enemy may be conceived of as someone with power and authority who oppresses us or as an alien who wages actual physical violence and

---

29 John 11: 11 and 35. The only other recorded examples of Jesus' tears were shed in lament over the coming fate of Jerusalem and in his agony before his death.

30 Matthew 26: 6; Mark 14: 13; Luke 19: 29; John 12: 1

war against us, the enemies that Jesus most often encountered were his equals within the religious community of his time.[31]

Jesus' teachings and behavior concerning enemies are quite different from those of the Hebrew scriptures. The psalms are filled with prayers seeking protection from one's enemies and revenge and retribution against them, even those with whom one had a close and intimate relationship. In the 41st psalm, for instance, protection and retribution are invoked against a best friend who had been trusted and then became a betrayer.[32]

Most of those who have betrayed me and turned against me and lied about me have been fellow members of the church, and pastoral counseling over the decades has convinced me that enemies within church relationships are not peculiar to those of us who are ordained ministers. Arguably Jesus' most difficult teachings were the mandates to "love your enemies, do good to those who hate you, bless those who curse you, pray for those who abuse you" and "love your enemies, doing good and expecting nothing in return." "If anyone strikes you on the cheek, offer the other also; and from anyone who takes away your coat do not withhold even your shirt."[33]

If the teachings of Jesus concerning our enemies challenges the very outer boundary of our humanity, his actions devastate our attempts at self-justification and excusing our behavior. Jesus taught us to pray to be able to forgive as we have been forgiven,[34] but at Calvary Jesus prayed for those who were crucifying him that they might be forgiven.[35] Here we reach both the summit and the uppermost limit of completed humanity, and we may well ask if such perfect humanity is even possible apart from the divine nature which was united to the human nature in the person of Christ. It may not be possible to think of the

---

31 The enemy that wages war and oppresses from a vantage of superior strength will be dealt with in a later section.

32 Psalm 41: 9-11, compare Psalm 55: 13-15

33 Luke 6: 27-28, 30, 35; compare Matthew 5: 43-44

34 Matthew 6: 12 and 14; Luke 11: 4

35 Luke 23: 34

human nature of Christ apart from his divine nature when we come
to the Cross; but even so, the ultimate example of true, full, complete
and perfect humanity is revealed for us only here, finally here, as we
look upon the crucified Lord *(kyrios)*.

# AUTOBIOGRAPHICAL VIGNETTES I

*The gynecologist told Rilla and me that with impediments in both our anatomies our chances of conceiving a child were 20,000 to one. It was before the era of in vitro fertilization, but before we started adoption procedures we were referred to a fertility expert in Birmingham. Dr. Thomas's methodology was perhaps more psychological than technical. When others said "impossible," he said all things are possible. When others counseled realism and discouragement, he offered hope and encouragement. Some surgical and medical remedies might be effective, but in the meantime he recommended tossing out the temperature charts and suggested some relaxed, comforting positions and occasions for making love.*

*At our next appointment with Dr. Thomas, when we were to have considered the surgical and medical options, Rilla told him about some of her recent symptoms. "My dear," he exclaimed, "You are pregnant." We went straight to Loveman's Department Store and bought Rilla a fur stole and had lunch in our favorite Chinese restaurant in celebration.*

*Rilla and I read a book and studied the Lamaze technique for natural childbirth. I was convinced that I could be a good coach during her labor—I was accustomed to seeing people in pain as a pastor in the hospital—but I was hesitant about delivery—I had often been affected by the sight of blood and had fainted when a surgeon insisted that I come into the operating room for the amputation of a leg during my Clinical Pastoral Education course.*

*The obstetricians in Selma, Alabama, had never participated in natural child birth and were reluctant to allow us to use it, but another woman had difficulty in the labor room, and the doctors observed us and were impressed. Despite several hours of labor, Rilla declined*

anesthesia; and when the moment for the delivery was imminent, Dr.
Blanton insisted that I put on a gown and come into the delivery room.
"You've done a great job so far helping with Rilla's labor, you've got to
see the climax." He was right. Rilla and I were both able to hold our
beautiful baby daughter as soon as she emerged from the womb. It was
a peak experience of my life (although ironically I could not touch the
baby again and saw her only through the glass window of the nursery
until Rilla was discharged, because the hospital regulations in those
days exiled fathers from the maternity ward when the babies were with
their mothers).

Lauren's birth was the most miraculous moment in our lives; but
the even greater miracle over time has been the bright, beautiful, loving
child, girl, woman, who has been our sublime delight for every year of
her life.

༄

During my first two years of college I rarely attended a local church
and often read a book during the sermon in my choir stall on Sunday
mornings at the Duke Chapel. I fancied myself to be something of an
agnostic; but during my junior year, as I became involved in the Civil
Rights Movement, I began to attend the Sunday evening services at Watts
Street Baptist Church. The pastor, Warren Carr, was a community leader
in fostering better race relations and made matters of faith seem real and
relevant to me. Sam Hill, then a graduate student in religion at Duke
and later Chair of the Religion Department at the University of North
Carolina, led a discussion for undergraduate students at Watts Street on
Sunday afternoons that would rival the learnedness of my later seminars
at Harvard Divinity School. I became involved in the Baptist Student
Union weekday programs on campus led by the Baptist chaplain, Bill
Smith, who provided the pastoral element of faith to the prophetic and
intellectual stimulation of Warren Carr and Sam Hill.

As my junior year progressed I started to doubt my intention of applying to law school and wondered if I should consider seminary. I asked
Bill Smith if he could arrange a summer internship in a more typical

*Baptist church than Watts Street but with a minister who shared some of my perspectives and concerns, so that I could make some vocational discernments. I was sent to Heflin, Alabama, where his best friend, Grady Jarrard, was the pastor. Although Heflin is not a great distance from my hometown in Georgia, I had never before set foot in Alabama, because our relatives all lived in Tennessee and South and North Carolina to the north and east.*

*My first day at work I asked Grady what he wanted me to do. "I want you to go down to the Post Office every morning at eight o'clock."*

*"To pick up the mail for the church?"*

*"No. The mail is delivered here at the church. I just want you to go down there for an hour every morning this week."*

*I thought the man was crazy, and this would be the shortest internship in history.*

*That week at the Post Office I met almost everyone in the town, and they met me. I learned a great deal about their joys and sorrows, their achievements and scandals, their human foibles and spiritual resources.*

*Four years later Grady preached the sermon—the "charge to the candidate" in Baptist parlance—at my ordination as a Baptist minister. He said that in negotiating all the currents of doctrine and all the controversies in congregational disputes never to forget to be a man and what it means to be human. His counsel may have been the first seed for this book, even though it took four and a half decades to germinate.*

⟡

*My Clinical Pastoral Education took place at the Dorothea Dix Hospital in Raleigh, North Carolina, the summer following my first year of seminary. After several days of orientation our group was assigned to various wards and buildings by the psychiatric team. I was sent to the building for the criminally insane. "Why are you sending me 'there'?" I asked "I'm the smallest guy in the class."*

*"That's part of the reason," I was told. "You won't intimidate the patients who won't feel threatened by you."*

*Therapy and diagnosis for the mentally ill have changed since the early 1960s. Thorazine was just being introduced as one of the first psycho tropic drugs, and shock therapy was still routinely administered—one of my most dreaded tasks was strapping and holding men down for it to be administered, although I didn't so much mind sitting with them as they were "coming out" from it, because they often told me things that helped me minister to them later. Homosexual activity was still against the law in North Carolina in those days, and several young men were committed to our care as "criminally insane" because they had been caught in sexual couplings.*

*Thus we had a broad spectrum of illnesses (and non-illnesses) in our building. The most violent of the "criminally insane," however, were housed in another, more secure ward. For the most part our patients were docile and often "spaced out," since the doctors were just beginning to learn the proper dosages for Thorazine. Even so, we had a double set of doors at the entrance to the building. To gain access you would unlock the first door, enter the vestibule, then lock the first door and unlock the inner door, except at times when the shifts of nurses and attendants were changing. Then to facilitate entering and leaving, one set of doors was left unlocked.*

*As I arrived for my shift early one morning I saw one of our patients wandering out on the lawn. Immediately I realized that both sets of doors had probably been left unlocked. The patient was a former mathematics professor from Wake Forrest University and was usually especially quiet and submissive. I thought I would simply take him by the hand and lead him back into the ward; but as soon as I took his hand, he began to choke me. He was a large man, twice my size and very strong. I thought I would surely be killed, but another attendant appeared at that moment and pulled him off me.*

*Part of my duty was supervising the morning cleanup of the dormitories. Many of the patients were held for what seemed to me, even then, to be silly and trivial offenses. I appealed to the psychiatrist in charge of our building to allow me to take some of the patients who were not judged to be psychotic to the canteen and recreation field on Saturdays as a reward after they had done their work well during the week, and he agreed.*

*One Saturday we were short staffed, and there was not another attendant free to take the men out with me. I barged into the psychiatrist's office and told him that it was "unconscionable"—one of my favorite words in those days—that the men would not be able to be rewarded as they had been promised. "Very well," he said, "if you think you can manage them, you can take them by yourself."*

*I swallowed my anxiety but wasn't about to back down. Our excursion to the canteen and their game of pitching balls to each other were uneventful—there were no epileptic seizures, which had been my greatest fear and which had occurred several times on our Saturday outings, requiring one person to attend the patient and another to watch everyone else.*

*The next morning the head nurse and psychiatrist in charge of our ward were waiting for me.*

*"Did you know that not all the patients returned with you yesterday?"*

*I have never been good at counting people—to prepare wafers for communion or determine the attendance to record in the parish register— especially if they are moving around.*

*"No, I had no idea. Who is missing?" I asked and didn't add the other question in my mind, 'And am I fired and dismissed from the CPE program?'*

*"Bob." He was a middle-aged man, one of the hardest working, most cooperative, most courteous patients on the ward; but I remembered almost dying at the hands of the professor and wondered if I had misjudged Bob, too.*

*"Were the police able to find him?"*

*"No, but he came back on his own last night."*

*"Before I have to leave, may I speak with him?"*

*I was granted permission to see Bob, who for some inexplicable reason always called me "Cap'n Miller."*

*"Bob, why did you leave me yesterday?"*

"Well, Cap'n Miller, when you was talking to some of the other men on the ball field and looking the other way I seen my chance to run, and I did."

"But, why, Bob?"

"Well, Cap'n Miller, I ain't seen a woman in close to seven-eight years now; and I wanted to have me a woman."

"I suppose I can understand that, but why did you come back last night?"

"Oh, Cap'n Miller, I couldn't leave all them beds for you to make up by yourself this morning, so after I had my time with a woman in town, I come on back."

It's a cliché, true like most clichés, that people who are crazy are not necessarily stupid. It's perhaps less often recognized that people who are mentally ill may also be unusually compassionate and kind and able to teach the rest of us much about what it means to be human.

We may also receive forgiveness and reconciliation from unlikely sources. I was not fired and dismissed from the program, although the psychiatrist may have been covering up his own liability for allowing me to take patients out by myself; but I never again took a group out of the building on a Saturday by myself that summer.

❧

Although we had lived in Alabama for several months I had never had the occasion to meet the pastor of Berea Baptist Church where some of Coretta Scott King's family were members. My earlier involvement in the Civil Rights Movement whetted my interest in becoming acquainted with this leader of the black community. Unlike most Baptist ministers he often wore a clerical collar; and one morning we arrived at the same time in the lobby of the Marion Bank and Trust Company, both wearing our clerical collars; and I saw my opportunity.

I walked up to the Rev. Mr. Johnson and boldly remarked, "I see you're another collared person." As soon as the words left my mouth I wished that the floor might open up and swallow me. Not knowing what else to do in my embarrassment and nervousness, I kept on talking; and Mr.

*Johnson's gracious dignity saved me from utter humiliation.*

*We became good friends. We worked to establish Marion's first Head Start program in his church, and I gave the address to the parents of the first graduating class. He participated in my daughter Lauren's baptism and was the last person to tell us goodbye with a farewell gift when we left Marion.*

∽

*After Lauren's miraculous birth our medical odds against having another child were still 20,000 to one. We considered adoption, but we were happy with our one beautiful child, and the long sequence of Rilla's health problems started. My nephews and the boys in my congregations over the years offered brief analogues of a father-son relationship, but two college students who accompanied me on a mission trip to Honduras became my most nearly surrogate sons.*

*Hank and Jonathan were good friends; and as good friends often are, they were quite different in personality and demeanor—Hank emotional, spontaneous, mercurial, endearing to everyone; Jonathan wary of deep commitment but steadfastly loyal once committed, reserved, reflective, thoughtful. Watching Jonathan progress in maturity from Peace Corps volunteer in Bolivia to Peace Corps director in Nicaragua, from graduate school student to husband has been a joy over many years. Officiating at his wedding with Lyana in Managua was an ecstatic day of pleasure in my life.*

*The weekend before he left to travel to India with a friend, Hank appeared unannounced at our house to "touch base," as he often did. I had qualms about the dangers of travel in India, but he made that leg of the journey safely. The morning of Lauren's graduation from the University of the South was another glorious time of ecstatic joy as her professors praised her intellect and accomplishments. Early that afternoon, when Rilla and I had returned to the motel to rest, Lauren burst into our room and fell weeping into my arms. "Enrique (what we called Hank) is dead." Returning from India during a stopover in Ireland, Hank had slipped on wet rocks at the beach and struck his head on a stone and died instantly. When his parents failed to reach me at home, they had called Lauren's telephone at the university. It was one of the darkest and most profoundly sad and sorrowful moments of my life, and all the more so because of the sudden plunge into the depths of despair from the morning's exultation. I grieved daily for Hank for many years, and the memory of his death still causes me painful sadness.*

*When Lauren married Neill I inherited a beloved and cherished son-in-law; and when Lennox was born I experienced the great thrill and joy of having a grandson; but as in the book of Job there would be no double portions in replaced progeny. Neill is my esteemed son-in-law, not my son; and Lennox is my adored grandson, not my son. Only Jonathan and Hank would be surrogate sons, one held in blessed memory and the other followed with a pride and affection closest to those of my own family.*

$$\sim$$

*Driving through an ice storm or leaving in the middle of the night after leading a Sunday service, I had always made it home for Christmas until my first year in Nicaragua. My house mate and most of my parishioners had left several days earlier for the United States. I was invited for a mid-afternoon dinner with friends, but on Christmas morning I was wallowing in twisted bed sheets and self-pity. When the telephone rang and the voice cooed, "This is the overseas operator in Miami," my heart raced in anticipation of a call from my family. Alas, it was a wrong number, and I blurted out my tale of woe to the hapless operator: how I was miserable in a foreign country, alone at Christmas for the first time in my life. About a half hour later the telephone rang again. "This is the overseas operator in Miami again. I'm having to work, and my family is way off, and I'm lonely, too. I thought we might chat a little."*

*Perhaps an hour later a taxi pulled up in front of the house. A taxi was extremely rare on any day in this colonia populated largely with American Embassy houses and an incredible aberration on Christmas Day. When I answered the doorbell, the driver handed me a little package covered in bright holiday paper and red bows with a note to "Little*

*Padre, who might feel lonely this Christmas. Sophie." Inside was a letter opener carved from Nicaraguan rosewood.*

*Sophie, an older British expatriate, owned the gift shop in the Gran Hotel in Managua and was the foulest mouthed woman I had ever met at that point in my young life. Unlike her older sister Melita who never missed a Sunday service, Sophie never came to church, even after cancer spread ominously through her body; but she accepted my prayers and expressions of concern with apparent gratitude in the back of her shop. When a colon resection and a colostomy bag and a remission arrested the cancer, she called me one morning to come down to her shop. I was afraid that the cancer had recurred; but when I came in the door she said, "I want you to have anything you want from my store for all you did for me when I was so sick." I told her that I didn't want anything from her, that I was happy to do what I did because it was my job and I loved her; but she insisted, and I realized it was important for her to give me something.*

*Sophie probably liked me more than other priests of her former acquaintance because I challenged her and wouldn't take any of her guff. At that moment I believed that Sophie needed challenging. "All right, Sophie, I want you to give me a pre-Colombian stone statue that's the real thing." Our glances probably communicated more than our words. I knew that most of the stone artifacts in her shop were fakes that she sold as the real thing. Pottery and textiles could be dated, but stone could easily be duplicated and would often remain undetected.*

*Her response with oaths and swear words that are unprintable in this book were followed by a plea. "You can have your choice of any other goddamn thing in this store that you want—jade, gold, pre-Colombian pottery—anything but that."*

*"Nope, Sophie, if you really want to give me something, I want a genuine pre-Colombian stone statue."*

*More curses, more swearing followed. "Okay, goddamnit; give me a couple of days."*

*I knew that if anyone could get a genuine stone artifact, Sophie could; and for my gift this time she would not even consider passing off a fake, although she would have sold me a copy as something over 500 years old in a heartbeat.*

*The pre-Colombian stone statue has had a place of honor on the mantel in every home where I have lived. I know it's genuine, although it can't be dated by any scientific test.*

∾

*At Christmas five years later in Nice, France, we were planning the final service in the American Church before we merged with the British Church for the beginning of the new year. The British Bishop of Fulham and Gibraltar had come for the event of the merger and was to celebrate the Eucharist at the Christmas midnight mass. He asked me how many communicants to expect, and I told him there would be about fifty, not more than seventy, because most of our members were elderly or had young children and would attend the twilight service (and didn't add that they were none too happy about the merger and wanted to hear my final sermon in the American Church).*

*That evening after the twilight service, however, a group of sailors from a U. S. naval ship that had just docked in Villefranche harbor knocked on my door. They asked if we were having a Christmas Eve service and told me they had formed a choir on the ship that had been practicing Christmas carols and would enjoy singing for our service. I didn't think that American sailors of various faiths and an English bishop would be a very good mix. I suggested that we delay the service for a quarter of an hour for them to give a concert on the chancel steps and told them my wife was an organist and might accompany them. After they rehearsed with Rilla I told them that if they were baptized Christians of whatever denomination they would be welcome to receive communion at our altar, and I demonstrated how it was done. That night as we passed 200 communicants and after reconsecrating twice the bishop sniffed and whispered to me, "Seventy at most indeed!"*

*We had not planned to have a reception after the service, but we invited the sailors over to share what we had. The wine was quickly exhausted, and I sent Michel out to buy whatever he could find in the wee hours of Christmas morning. He returned with boxes of powered milk and cocoa; and we made hot chocolate, which the sailors seemed to enjoy even more than the wine—at least there was plenty of it.*

*I had not forgotten my first Christmas away from home in a foreign land, and on a whim I told the sailors that they could make a telephone call to their families in the States on my tab. I had an egg timer glass with sand that dribbled into the bottom after three minutes before it was turned back over. I asked them not to exceed the three minutes, and not a single one of them did.*

*The next week several of our teenagers were in my office, and I called Canon Hearsey at the English Church to ask if we could bring over the desks and books and art supplies for Sunday School. The English Church had almost no children, and we had a large number of children. The British were both enthusiastic and terrified about being invaded by the Americans, especially by our children, and none more so than Canon Hearsey, who had taught me much about liturgy and Anglican worship and tradition. The merger had been forced on the British community in Nice as much as on the American by the powers that be in New York and London.*

*"Oh, John, are we beginning Sunday School this Sunday?"*

*"Yes, Canon Hearsey, we've said the whole church program would begin with the first Sunday of the merger."*

*A deep sigh. "Oh, John, must we . . . so soon?"*

*"I believe we must. That's what we've published and told the people."*

*Another deeper sigh. "Well, if we must, we must."*

*And on that note of enthusiasm our merger began.*

━◦ঌ◦━

*No road connected the west and east coasts of Nicaragua between the Pacific and the Atlantic Oceans. The road ended in Rama where you could take a boat down the Rio Escondido to Bluefields. (Rio Escondido means "Hidden River," in part because legend avers that pirates hid their treasure along the banks of its many crooks in centuries past when the*

*Spanish and the English challenged each other on the high seas, with not always very savory characters.) The lazy voyage over the brown water allowed plenty of opportunity to see banana and pineapple and mahogany and teak plantations and observe kingfishers and herons and cormorants and various shore birds.*

*Rama was open range country without much law enforcement. A few rooms with tijeras (scissors-like folding cots) were available for the night over the saloon, which actually featured swinging doors through which the cowboys passed at sunset, sometimes firing off their pistols to celebrate the end of their day's labor. I was not comfortable letting my recently wedded blonde wife spend the night in Rama, but I wanted her to see the countryside and the river when we went to Bluefields for a conference. So it was we made the grueling trip in one eighteen hour day, leaving Managua in the dark before sunrise and arriving in Bluefields in the deep darkness of the night hours after the few electric lights of the town had been extinguished. The confluence of Nature and history seemed to meld as we crossed the continent from one ocean to another overland (and over water) in a single day.*

*The year I was scheduled to give the keynote address at the diocesan convention in Bluefields, I decided to fly from Managua. Rilla chose not to make that journey again. Episcopalians in Nicaragua were concentrated on the east (Atlantic) coast in Bluefields and Puerto Cabezas and many small villages. (Years later I made an appointment on a trip back to Nicaragua to visit with the Rt. Rev. Sturdie Downs, longtime Episcopal Bishop of Nicaragua. I told him how much I'd looked forward to meeting him after missing connections several times in the United States. Bishop Downs told me that we had already met; he had heard me give the convention address when he was a teenager in Bluefields.)*

*Rilla picked me up at the airport in Managua on my return flight from Bluefields and told me as soon as I got into the car, "I have some bad news. I had a hit and run accident with an ox cart."*

*"Rilla! You hit an ox cart and left the scene of the accident!"*

*"No, you don't understand. The ox cart hit our car and sped away."*

*The image of an ox cart speeding away is difficult to imagine, but on the narrow dirt road to our home, where we then lived deep in the campo on a finca owned by a French family, it was not possible to turn around without driving for perhaps several miles. I had instructed Rilla whenever she met an ox cart to pull as far as possible to the side of the road, and the ox cart driver would get off and carefully lead the oxen around her. This time, however, a young boy about ten years old clucked the oxen onward; and the axle of the cart scraped the side of our Volkswagen bug.*

*As soon as Rilla could turn around, she returned to our house and called Carlos, our teenaged gardener. "Did you get the tag number?" he asked her.*

*"I didn't know ox carts had tag numbers."*

*Rilla and Carlos sped off to find the hit and run culprit. When they found him, he had reached his father and uncles who were drunk from attending the wake of someone who had just died. Carlos began to upbraid the boy and tell him he would have to pay to repair the car. The older men became indignant, and Rilla began to realize that she was in a vulnerable position with her husband on the other coast and only a teenaged gardener in the house to protect her. She called Mr. Grimm, our appropriately named German insurance agent, whom we paid more to keep us out of harm's way than to repair our cars. He came out and pacified the men but warned the little boy about proper procedures for driving an ox cart in the future; and, of course, we paid the body shop for the repairs out of our own pocket.*

*Carlos and Emmalina, our housekeeper, were ever ready to defend us and protect us. When an earthquake or a coup or a hurricane struck, even before I became aware of the danger, they would have risen before dawn to lay in a supply of rice and beans and bananas and plantain and candles and fill every vessel in the house with water. When Carlos or Emmalina or Martín (later our church custodian) or Tana (later our housekeeper when we moved) were ill and had health issues, we obtained for them the medicines and care that they could not have afforded or accessed on their own. When they accumulated debts that they could not repay—seemingly enormous to them, paltry to us—we paid them.*

*In almost four decades since leaving Nicaragua the social organization of the places I have lived differ greatly from Central America, but in all of them there has also been a complex network of trust and interdependency which is a mark of any community that is truly human.*

                                             ∿

*A clergyman shares the weal and woe of many people every year—critical illnesses, births, deaths, marriages, divorces, family conflicts, lawsuits, bankruptcies, imprisonments—and over a span of years perhaps several such dramatic events in the same family. We do not serve career-long cures in recent years as often as in previous centuries. I was privileged to prepare parents for confirmation, baptize and marry their children and present them for confirmation and baptize their grandchildren for only one family, because they followed me to parishes in different towns.*

*With no other family, however was I involved in such dramatic events as with Dick and Alice Pfeiffer. Alice was reared in Nicaragua, where her father had been an engineer in the country's gold mines. Dick was a Californian, educated in North Carolina, who came to Nicaragua as a recent college graduate in agronomy with a few dollars in his pocket and an idea for beginning a cotton industry.*

*By the time I met Dick and Alice they had four children and had attained considerable wealth. Alice took me shopping to set up my church office when I first arrived in Managua. I enjoyed being included in their simple family suppers and admired the efficient and unpretentious ways they guided their children's lives. Dick enjoyed singing in the choir with the greatest gusto I've ever seen in a man. Alice helped to organize the Sunday School. The Sunday bulletins and monthly newsletters and all other letters and published materials for the church were prepared and printed by Dick's company. Dick and Alice were probably the largest contributors to the Union Church budget (although I have never known precisely what my members give financially in any of my parishes).*

*Dick and Alice thought their family was complete with two girls and two boys all in school, when they were surprised and delighted to learn that Alice was pregnant. The beautiful baby, "Miss Annie," was her parents' and siblings' cosseted darling.*

*Whenever a baby was baptized at the Union Church I asked Wolfram Fliegel, the Moravian missionary, to perform the actual ritual after I offered prayers. Wolfram was one of Dick's closest friends, and I assumed Dick would be happy for him to baptize Anne. Not so. Dick and Alice said I was their pastor, and they wanted me to baptize her. I told them how it violated my identity as an ordained Baptist minister and my understanding of the Union Church as interdenominational rather than non-denominational as we each preserved our American church affiliations abroad. They were unyielding and asked me to think and pray about it. After much prayer and thought I realized that I had already moved away from my Baptist sacramental theology, and I agreed to baptize their baby. People have often asked me if it was a difficult and agonizing decision to move from the Baptist to the Episcopal ministry, and I always tell them that deciding to baptize Anne Pfeiffer posed much greater difficulty and agony and that comparatively changing denominations was relatively easy.*

*When "Miss Annie" was two years old each member of her family thought she was with one of the others, and she fell into the family's swimming pool and drowned. She was the first baby I had ever baptized and the first I buried. The preparation for funerals in Nicaragua is quite different from that in the United States. I went with Dick to buy the plot for the burial in the cemetery and hire the gravediggers and cut the rope to lower the casket into the ground. I watched Alice and her older daughters and their maids wash and anoint Anne's body and dress her. As described to me by Wolfram and other clergymen who had lived for years in Nicaragua, I thought they were cruel procedures; but I learned they were merciful exercises for working through grief and sorrow.*

*Several years later the weather and international markets conspired to devastate the cotton industry in Central America. Dick's colleagues sold out for what they could get and returned to the United States, but Dick was unwilling to leave until he could restore the holdings of the small Nicaraguan farmers who contracted with him. I went to see him and suggested that a church pledge is not a contract, and he shouldn't feel bound by it in the present circumstances. He told me that for him it was a sacred vow, and he would honor it at least until his family was in need of food. Eventually Dick restored his business. The Pfeiffers left Nicaragua only after the revolution under the Sandinistas but without the anger and bitterness of other expatriates who had sought their fortunes in Nicaragua.*

*My parents had never flown in an airplane before they came to visit me in Managua. My father had taught agricultural classes for much of his life; and when Dick flew him across Lake Managua in his small private airplane to see his farms, it was one of the great thrills of Dad's latter years.*

*A few years ago Dick and Alice came to visit us in Alabama. They had given birth to another daughter a few years after Anne's death; and they brought Patricia to Alabama to meet our daughter Lauren, about her age. We heard about the lives of the four older, now grown children; and we learned about another connection of our lives never before revealed to either of us.*

*Nicaragua during the Somoza era could be a dangerous place. It was rumored that some men who opposed the government were thrown into a volcano. A visitor from Panama to our home once cautioned me about speaking openly regarding my political views, because he could be an informant for the Somoza regime. When a young Roman Catholic priest, who had recently arrived in the country, learned that powerful members of the government had taken young boys from the streets and kept them in a house to serve as slaves for their sexual perversions, he began talking openly about the atrocity. A member of the Union Church learned that the young priest's life was threatened and that he was in serious peril of being murdered. My parishioner (who was married to a devout Roman Catholic), was afraid to go to the Roman Catholic hierarchy of the country, because, although many of them were good and honorable priests, some were in league with the governmental officials; and if information should be passed along in gossip, it could further imperil the young priest's life. It was determined that I would meet the priest quite publicly at the coffee shop of the Gran Hotel, chat for a while, and then drive him, apparently casually to a designated spot. It would be assumed that we were on the way to some church meeting and so we would probably not be followed. I was not to know who would pick him up. None of us in the chain knew who the others were for our mutual protection in case any of us were taken into custody. We would then work behind the scenes to free the child sex slaves. I knew only that the plan involved eventually getting the priest across the northern border into Honduras. It was the only experience in my life with "cloak and dagger" espionage.*

*Somehow the story came up as Dick and Alice sat in our living room in Montgomery over two decades later. "So you were a part of that scheme, too," we exclaimed in effect to each other. Someone had picked up the priest where I had left him and taken him to Dick's plane. Dick had flown him across the lake, as he had flown my father a few months before; and after nightfall he was taken over the border into Honduras.*

*Some rare and beloved people cross and recross our lives and deepen our sense of what humanity means with each intersection.*

❦

*After I had submitted my resignation to the churches in Managua, the Most Rev. John Hines made the first tour of Central America by a Presiding Bishop of the American Episcopal Church, and I was his chauffeur in Managua. He asked me to hold myself open for a special short-term assignment, which he could not describe to me yet for confidential reasons. I assumed the job would involve Latin American programs at our church headquarters in New York City, but it turned out that he wanted me to go to Nice, France, to work with the merger of American Episcopal and Church of England parishes. I had no background in French culture or language, but my years of working with a diverse English speaking expatriate community seemed to have aroused his interest.*

*The reason for his secrecy was that the Rt. Rev. Edmond Browning, who would later be elected as the Presiding Bishop himself, was in process of being appointed Bishop of the American Convocation of Episcopal*

Churches in Europe and was traveling from Japan by way of the Trans-Siberian Railroad; but his new position could not yet be announced.

For two weeks I lived with Bishop Browning and his family. Bishop Browning had served the American Church in Nice during the summer as its parish priest before my arrival, in great part because the Rectory was large enough for his wife, five children, and Japanese au pair. The Rectory, built and furnished by members of the Vanderbilt family, contained some of Queen Victoria's antiques that they had acquired when she gave up her lodgings on the Riviera due to advancing age. It was like living in a museum, interesting and challenging; but greater than the interest and challenge of bishops and museum quartering were the French housekeeper and verger who had been attached to the church for over forty years.

Louise was less than five feet tall; but she ruled the house (much as Emmalina had ruled my house in Managua; she had refused to let my mother into her kitchen while visiting me). Louise had refused to give the key to the chest of antique silver flatware to Patty Browning, the bishop's wife. Patty had to request that it be opened before each dinner party or reception. In the top of the chest Louise had placed a list of each piece of missing silver and under which priest's tenure it had disappeared. (When the Brownings were driving out the gate to take up their permanent residence in Germany, I rushed out waving my arms. When Patty rolled the car window glass down to see what was the matter, I told her that if she had a silver fork in her luggage, she'd better hand it over now, because I didn't want it recorded in the lid of the chest on my watch. Years later we laughed about my impudence toward a bishop's—and future presiding bishop's—wife.) Louise immediately gave Rilla the key to the silver chest. Patty didn't speak French and had five children; Rilla spoke French and at that time we had no children capable of misplacing pieces of silver. Michel and Louise had buried the household silver and communion vessels and some of the brass from the church in the back garden when Nazi officers confiscated the Rectory for their living quarters during World War II.

When we were out at night for a concert or a dinner party, Michel *would wait up for us, no matter how late our return, to run out and open the driveway gate after the car lights appeared. It annoyed me enormously. I told him over and over again that I was perfectly capable of getting out of the car and opening the gate for myself, but my protests were to no avail. I felt like a teenager being monitored for his curfew by a parent, but in time I came to understand it as Michel's devotion to duty and faithful service.*

*We wanted to treat Michel and Louise to a special dinner at one of Nice's best restaurants before we left. Like all French people they valued fine cuisine above almost everything else in life. They would promise to go and set a date and then cancel, time after time. Finally, they said they couldn't both leave because their little dog would cry; but we saw through their subterfuge: in forty years both of them had never left the church unattended; one of them had always been present to keep it safe.*

*After all plans were in place to close the American Church and merge with the British Church, where all services and activities would hence-forth be conducted, Bishop Browning came from Germany especially to meet with Michel and Louise and assure them that they would receive a pension adequate to maintain them for as long as they lived. Bishop Browning also spoke no French, and Rilla translated for him. Michel was large and round and weighed perhaps three times as much as Louise. He sat awkwardly and nervously during the conversation. When Bishop Browning finished telling them the details about their pension, he asked, through Rilla, if they had any questions.*

*"Oh, yes, Monseigneur, will I still be allowed to change the frontals on the altar for each saint's day, even when there are no longer services in the church?"*

*"Ye watchers and ye holy ones . . . ."*
*#618, Latin 5th-8th Century,*
*The Episcopal Hymnal, 1982*

༄

*The college mission team, which included Hank and Jonathan and my daughter Lauren, had been a great success as we demonstrated a* several day youth retreat at the new diocesan camp in Honduras. I always tried to design projects that would not take jobs away from local nationals and would contribute something that they could not easily do for themselves. Then everything fell apart.

Muchilena, the diocesan camp, was located on a peninsula near the Guatemalan border. In the heavy rains at the end of the week a flood cut the peninsula off from the mainland. We were stranded on a small "island" without food or provisions with over twenty young children. The team huddled and discussed how the vagaries of nature and poverty prevented Hondurans from precise planning for the future. It was a lesson in trusting God; but it was only the beginning of our learning. One of the teachers from the orphanage that was home to the young girls on our retreat had bought fish and vegetables to take back to the city for her family. Without telling us, she cooked them into a stew and fed all of us with an ample and delicious feast that sustained us until we could get across the flood. Although I could not replace her provision, I offered to reimburse her at least for her expenditures; but she declined saying we had taught and given them much and this was her gift to us.

Because we were delayed more than thirty-six hours the reservations for our van and our hotel at the Mayan Ruins were canceled. We secured an old U. S. yellow school bus, recycled as a public transport in Honduras long after its useful life had ended and made an agonizingly slow trip groaning at less than twenty miles an hour up mountainsides to Copán. We found lodging in a primitive guest house with lattice walls in the front, which one of the girls, who had never traveled far from southern Alabama, in a shrill voice described as "only that 'lettuce' between us and those guerillas," after she'd heard gunfire during the night.

After we finished our formal study of Mayan history in Copán some of the students who had extra vacation time accompanied me to Roatán in the Bay Islands off the Honduran coast for a snorkeling adventure. The pouring rain continued every day. Then an emergency call from the bishop's office alerted me that the national airline on which he held tickets had just gone into bankruptcy.

At Copán and Roatán there was scant trace of the panic and fear we *had experienced on Muchilena, however, because our Honduran friends had taught us something about patience and endurance and putting our trust in God and had shown us how divine mercy often comes through the agency of human generosity.*

# Discerning Our Human Identity in History

*"The first man, Adam, became a living being"; the last Adam became a life-giving spirit.* — I CORINTHIANS 15: 45 (NRSV)

*. . . Adam . . . is a type of the one who is to come.* — ROMANS 5: 14 (NRSV)

Adam is the mythic progenitor of humanity, and Adam is a type for Christ; but for people of faith biblical history begins with Abraham. If we are all children of Adam according to mythological biology, we are children of Abraham according to historical faith. Although some scholars believe that Abraham represents a tribe or an aggregation of individuals whose religious consciousness evolved over time, I prefer to believe that Abraham was a historical figure in a particular era of human history. Whether he was a discreet individual or not, however, Abraham represents a break in the chronology of religion in the biblical narrative as well as a distinction from other religious traditions.

The children of Abraham affirm three tenets of faith that distinguish them from other religions and thus define for them a great part of what it means to be human: God can be personally known and experienced and actively encountered and engaged; God is supremely powerful and ultimately victorious over all other gods and forces in the universe; and God is righteous and requires us to imitate divine righteousness. Whether Abraham was a strict monotheist, indeed whether Christianity is strictly monotheistic, may be debated, although Islam and even modern Judaism are more unambiguously monotheistic. Unlike Jews and Muslims, most Christians cannot claim even a symbolic physical descent from Abraham through Isaac or Ishmael, but Christians join the adherents of the other two great Abrahamic religions to claim a spiritual descent by faith and adherence to the three great distinguishing principles.[1]

Being human involves a consciousness (or a denial) of deity. To be human requires one to wrestle with the possibility of God. The particular consciousness of God first exhibited in Abraham was developed through following centuries of Hebrew history, and, Christians believe, perfectly fulfilled in Jesus. The very first verse of the New Testament identifies Jesus as the son of Abraham (as well as the son of David and Messiah, which will be discussed later).[2]

In addition to the distinguishing characteristics of religious sensibility, part of the discernment of our humanity involves how we interpret our heritage from Abraham. The promise to Abraham that his descendants will be as numerous as the stars of the heavens and the grains of sand on the seashore and even more importantly that he and his descendants will inherit the land and become a great nation and that all nations will be blessed (or bless themselves) in him is variously understood between and even within the different Abrahamic traditions of faith.[3] This promise is reaffirmed and claimed in the New Testament by Christians in the Songs of Mary and Zechariah and the confession of Stephen at his martyrdom.[4] The promise and descent of Jesus from Abraham are also explicitly enunciated in Peter's response to the Jewish leaders in the Temple.[5] And the book of Hebrews observes that Jesus came not to "help angels, but the descendants of Abraham."[6]

Whether this promised blessing is a literal physical inheritance or a spiritual inheritance or both sharply divides adherents within Juda-

---

1   See Matthew 3: 9; Luke 3: 8
2   Matthew 1: 1
3   Genesis 12: 2-3; 15: 5-6
4   Luke 1: 55 & 73; Acts 7: 17
5   Acts 3: 13 & 25
6   Hebrews 2: 16

ism, Christianity, and Islam from each other and from one another within each religion and may be tangentially related to the issues of the physical or spiritual descent from Abraham noted above. Jesus and Paul seem to express positions affirming both material and spiritual inherited blessings and both physical and spiritual descent from Abraham but with enough ambiguity to result in conflicting claims among Christians.

It is perhaps not too great an exaggeration to say that for Christians how we assess the role of Abraham indicates the way we regard historical lineage as an element of our humanity. Jesus recognized the privilege of Abrahamic descent in addressing Zacchaeus and in responding to those who criticized him for healing a crippled woman on the sabbath, asking if they were not respectively a son or a daughter of Abraham and so deserving of salvation.[7] He noted (perhaps pedagogically) the precedence of the children of Israel before healing the daughter of a Syrophoenician woman[8] and instructed his disciples to go nowhere among the Gentiles but go rather to the "lost sheep of the house of Israel."[9] Abraham, as well as Moses, are revered in his parables of Dives and Lazarus.[10] Yet, in one of his sternest rebukes to both Saducees and Pharisees, Jesus denigrated the presumption of privilege by descent from Abraham and implicitly established the basis of the spiritual descent from Abraham that was fully developed by Paul. " . . . don't say to yourselves, 'We have Abraham as our ancestor'; for I tell you from these stones God is able to raise up children to Abraham."[11]

For Paul the issue of descent from Abraham becomes a basic motif of human identity. If we find ambiguity in Jesus, we discover ambivalence in Paul. The appeal to the advantage of his own Abrahamic ancestry may have been played by Paul for his strategic advantage depending on the situation, much as he was not reluctant to use his Roman

---

7    Luke 13: 16 & 19: 9
8    Mark 7: 27
9    Matthew 10: 6
10   Luke 16: 22-31
11   Matthew 3: 9; Luke 3: 8

citizenship for a similar advantage in a different situation.[12] Yet, Paul's agenda for including Gentiles in the household of faith and somehow attaching them to biblical promises resulted in elaborate arguments and justifications for spiritual descent from Abraham. After a long explication in the Galatian letter detailing descendence through faith and righteousness, Paul concludes, "If you belong to Christ, then you are Abraham's offspring, heirs according to the promise."[13] He reiterates in Romans that "the promise may rest on grace and be guaranteed to all his descendants, not only to the adherents of the law, but also to those who share the faith of Abraham . . . ."[14] Although Paul's purpose is the inclusion of Gentile Christians in the promise to Abraham, it should be noted he does not claim they replace the Hebrews of physical descent: ". . . has God rejected his people? By no means! I myself am an Israelite, a descendant of Abraham, a member of the tribe of Benjamin."[15] Paul is not always consistent or evenhanded in his inclusion of the Jews, but a case could be made that he might also have included Muslims as Abraham's physical heirs to certain divine promises through Ismael, "the child born according to the flesh," if we stretch his somewhat fanciful and inconsistent analogies.[16]

For both Jesus and Paul the descendence and promise derived from Abraham, both physical and spiritual, are important in discerning a human identity; but they are of secondary importance. The human identity given by history may be imagined in three ascending levels of priority. First, we acknowledge our physical ancestors and the material benefits we have received from them as our inheritance in recognition that our humanity belongs to a larger community than our immediate personal circle and is rooted in a past of generations and centuries before the present time. Second, we affirm the values and truths and ethics as well as the spiritual lore that have been passed down to us

---

12 Galatians 1: 14; Acts 22: 25-26; and especially II Corinthians 11: 22
13 Galatians 3: 29; See also Galatians 3: 6-29
14 Romans 4: 16
15 Romans 11: 1
16 Galatians 4: 24-30

by them, whether or not we are literal biological descendants or even
racially, ethnically, or nationally related to those giants of the past.
And third, as Christians we finally confess that our primary human
identity is derived from Jesus himself, who proclaims, "Very truly I tell
you, before Abraham was, I am."[17] In John's Gospel the ambiguity of
respect and reverence for Abraham's physical descendants in contrast
to the inner truth of following Abraham spiritually is greatly elabo-
rated. When Jesus exposes the plot to kill him, he first acknowledges
his accusers as "descendants of Abraham"; but then he tells them that
if they were "Abraham's children," they would be doing what Abraham
did and not trying to kill him.[18]

In discerning our human identity we must explore the relative priorities of physical descent and spiritual descent not only from biblical
ancestors but also from our more recent familial and national ancestors and then subject them both to the true and complete example of
humanity in Jesus.

When I was four years old my paternal grandfather died and we
left the "dream home" my parents had built on the northern end of the
Keith farm and moved into the rambling twelve room farm house with
my grandmother. Although large and imposing in appearance from the
outside, the old house build by my grandfather and other men from
the farm was at best rustic inside. The only functional bathroom was
framed onto a corner of the back porch near the kitchen. (An upstairs
toilet and sink without hot water were used only in the summer so
that the pipes would not freeze.) During the years we lived with my
grandmother, my brother and sister were born. The older members
of my grandmother's family and my mother's family linked me to the
lore and legends of previous generations. Occasionally I would hear
stories from those whose names appeared on the tombstone of the

---

17 John 8: 58

18 John 8: 37-40 The word in this passage for descendant is *sperma*, literally "seed";
but the phrase for "Abraham's child" is *tekva tou Abraham*, "literally a child in relation to father and mother." p. 815, W. F. Arndt and F. W. Gingrich, *A Greek-English
Lexicon of the New Testament and Other Early Christian Literature*, University of
Chicago, revised edition, 1957

family cemetery across the road from "the big house" where we lived, but it was much later in life that I explored their genealogy.

Sunday afternoons were spent more often than not visiting in the homes of one of my grandmother's eight brothers and sisters, all of whom lived nearby, and on occasional Sundays as well as during the Thanksgiving and Christmas holidays at my maternal grandfather's home. My grandmother's family, the Quarles, descended from Appalachian mountain stock. Even though many of them had received some college education, they spoke with the ungrammatical hillbilly twang that only much later I learned was at times close to an antiquated British Elizabethan dialect. (The Keiths as well as the Latimers, Dupres, and Dobbs, my mother's kin, spoke a more conventional proper English.) To the Quarles the righteousness of faith was conveyed by the way you treated others, especially children and the elderly and the poor and sick, both human and animals. They tended to be suspicious of fancy talk about being good. They attended church services regularly, although not necessarily weekly, because the country Baptist congregation met only once or twice a month; but they rarely spoke or even sang—leaving that to other people—except for an occasional "Amen," when they especially agreed with the preacher. In their own homes, however, they spoke openly and often loudly about the faults and failings, as well as achievements and successes of extended family members, usually with great care and concern and stratagems for remedy, only rarely about other families, unlike the Keiths' and Latimers' and Dobbs' and Dupres' whispered secrets that were meant to elude (but nevertheless always reached) the ears of children. Bodily functions, even sexual ones, were addressed with equal candor, again in marked contrast to my other older relatives. My Great Grandfather Quarles distrusted newfangled automobiles and still rode his horse down to our house, as stiff as a ramrod in his eighties. He seemed the embodiment of an oak of righteousness.

The Quarles were also great story tellers recounting the foibles of members of previous generations as well as the stumblings of the present generation, especially those of us who were young, amidst loud and raucous laughter. Their teasing was always good natured, never cruel or malicious, and seasoned with compliments and folksy advice. The stories about Aunt Lean, their own maiden aunt of a previous generation, affirmed the continuity of their characters and characteristics. The alcoholism of one uncle and his sons was acknowledged regretfully and openly, but not made to seem an unforgivable sin and always accompanied by references to their generosity. From the Quarles I witnessed a pattern of Abrahamic righteousness and learned that true righteousness is best tempered by humor, balance and compassion.

The Latimers, and to a lesser extent the Dobbs and Dupres, were as emotional, sentimental and vocal about their religious and moral beliefs as the Quarles were stoic and unsentimental. They loved to sing hymns, and many of the Dupres were especially remarkable musicians. In their pronouncements, if not always in their behavior, righteousness was a matter of articulated right and wrong, as if black and white with no shade of gray. They possessed an aesthetic sense almost foreign to the Quarles and added a vision of the beauty of righteousness to that of the rectitude of righteousness.

A kind of gender reversal is evident between my familial ancestors and biblical ancestors. The bearers of lore and tradition and articulated righteousness in my family were mostly women, although their stories of previous generations were almost equally about both women and men. Most of the stories of the Bible focus on men, too; but Miriam and Hannah and Ruth and Esther from the Hebrew scriptures and Mary, the mother of Jesus, and Mary Magdalene in the Gospels are such vivid characters that I could imagine them in the company of my great aunts, supreme examples of faithfulness. One facet of righteousness is surely the faithfulness over years and generations which would seem more often evidenced in women than in men, in both my family and in the biblical narrative. In supporting the frailty of children or the elderly, in ministering to the ill and infirm, in encouraging the disconsolate and dying, these women appeared at the appropriate moments, even at Calvary, and exhibited the enduring faithfulness in righteousness that is perfectly revealed in Jesus.

Because my paternal grandfather died when I was four years old, we rarely saw members of the extended Keith family from his generation; and I did not hear the family legends and biographies about the Keiths, as I did about the Quarles and Latimers and Dobbs and Dupres. As a middle-aged adult I became interested in the genealogy and ancestry of the Keith family; and in addition to tracing the stories of nine generations in America, I became acquainted with the origins and history of the Keiths in Scotland and came to know three generations of the Earls of Kintore, the chiefs of Clan Keith, and their families.

From these stories I gained an impression of people who take risks for a greater good and become pioneers and explorers of new worlds and new enterprises. Jesus' parables about risking everything for the pearl of great value and the hidden treasure came alive for me through the tales of my Keith ancestors. These impressions were amplified by research into the first generations of the Keiths in America during the 18th Century: Cornelius who arrived in Virginia in 1709 from Scotland and who migrated to the wilderness and ran the first ferry across the Roanoke River (and also served as a Lay Reader for Anglicans in the region), his son who migrated to North Carolina and grandson who migrated to South Carolina and great grandson (my great great great grandfather) who finally reached Georgia, all in "search of a better country."[19]

These biographies together with their embellished stories and legends led me to seek for the one whom the book of Hebrews calls the "pioneer and perfecter of our faith."[20] Even before his final journey to Jerusalem, Jesus took risks and crossed borders into hostile territory for a greater good and purpose. He traveled through Samaria and even interacted with Samaritans, when other contemporary rabbis and Jewish leaders avoided that region.[21] As he approached Jerusalem, even his disputants warned him to flee from Herod who wanted to kill him, but

---

19 Hebrews 11: 16
20 Hebrews 12: 2
21 Luke 9: 52; 17: 11-19; John 4: 1-42

Jesus went forward steadfastly toward his goal and purpose.[22]

Awareness of the fullness of our humanity requires an understanding of its limitations and its possibilities. In biblical tradition the polarities of limitation and possibility are often expressed as law and freedom. Moses, the lawgiver, dominates the Hebrew scriptures and remains an archetype in the New Testament. One of the dominant characteristics of Abrahamic faith—that God is righteous and requires us to imitate divine righteousness—receives a definite expression as it is codified by Moses, who is always regarded as the symbolic, if not necessarily the literal, author and receptor of the statutes and commandments that have been received from God. The Hebrew prophets and Jesus and the New Testament evangelists and epistolers all wrestle with the role of the law; but when they raise the issues about the conflict between law and freedom, they question the particular codification of the law, not the limits and obligations on humanity that is the essence of the divine law.

Jesus is at least implicitly represented in the New Testament as the new lawgiver. Many scholars believe that Matthew structured his gospel in five sections imitating the five books of the Pentateuch. In his prologue John says that the law was given through Moses but grace and truth came through Jesus Christ;[23] and the book of Hebrews expresses the belief that Jesus was more worthy of glory than Moses.[24] No one before or perhaps ever since, however, has struggled more with the tension between law and freedom than Paul.[25]

However radically the codification of the law may be reinterpreted or even replaced, the role of the law is never denied, and Moses remains as its template. Time after time Jesus refers to the Mosaic codification of the law in addressing quandaries of divorce and family relationships

---

22 Luke 13: 31-33

23 John 1: 17

24 Hebrews 3: 3

25 See, for example, Romans 7: 1-7

and responsibilities,[26] as well as ritual obligations.[27] Jesus affirmed his role in fulfilling, not abolishing, the law and the prophets and implied that the law would not pass away until God's kingdom was perfectly fulfilled at the end of human time.[28] Jesus even urged people to follow what the scribes taught in their interpretation of the Mosaic law, although to be wary of imitating their often hypocritical behavior;[29] and the Risen Christ on the Emmaus Road led two disciples to an understanding of the meaning of the resurrection by beginning with the tradition from Moses.[30] The two figures that appeared on the mountain at Jesus' transfiguration were not Abraham and David, whose son he was called, but rather Moses, the lawgiver, and Elijah, who represented the prophetic interpretation of the law.[31]

A rabbi colleague in Montgomery, Alabama, helped me to understand how the law represents for the Jewish people the actual mediated divine presence on earth. I could never read Psalm 119 in the same way again after my conversations with Mark Biller. The law was not just the requirement and direction given by God for righteousness, it was more nearly God's very presence in word and concept directing people to an imitation of divine righteousness. That understanding of the Jewish reverence for the divine law led me to a fuller understanding of the radical New Testament claims about Jesus. Beginning with the synoptic gospels and spelled out by John and Paul, Jesus is portrayed neither merely as a reinterpreter of the law nor even as a new lawgiver but rather the new embodiment of the law itself. Jesus does not tell us, in the words of John, what are the grace and truth that we follow toward an imitation of divine righteousness, he is the embodiment of that very grace and truth.[32] In John's gospel Jesus says, "If you believed

---

26  Matthew 8: 4; 19: 7-8; 22: 24; 23: 2; Mark 7: 10
27  Matthew 8: 4
28  Matthew 5: 17-18; Luke 16: 17
29  Matthew 23: 2
30  Luke 24: 27
31  Matthew 17: 4; Mark 9: 4-5; Luke 9: 30-33
32  John 1: 14

Moses, you would believe me, for he wrote about me."[33] And in his usual mixed metaphorical-allegorical manner Paul writes about seeing divine righteousness through a veil in the old covenant, *i.e.,* the law, but seeing it directly (unveiled) in Christ.[34]

In a way Jesus "un-codified" the law. In what came to be called "the summary of the law," Jesus defines the two great commandments as love of God and love of neighbor.[35] But does the mandate to love God and love neighbor give any more guidance than the Abrahamic mandate to imitate divine righteousness, which Jesus also reiterates in Matthew's version saying, "Be perfect as your heavenly Father is perfect";[36] and in Luke's version saying, "Be merciful as your Father is merciful"?[37] In both gospels this general mandate follows Jesus' interpretations and clarifications of the Mosaic law in particular situations.

While the "summary of the law," loving God with all your heart and with all your soul and with all your mind and with all your strength,[38] and loving your neighbor as yourself can be thought of as a reinterpretation of the law, at the Last Supper according to John's Gospel, Jesus explicitly gives a new commandment: "I give you a new commandment, that you love one another. Just as I have loved you, you also should love one another."[39] The radical change in this new commandment comes by imitating Jesus who embodies the law rather than in discovering different interpretations or new commandments for particular situations. Paul echoed this changed perspective in his counsel to the Christians in Corinth "to be imitators of me, as I am of Christ."[40] Although Jesus

---

33 John 5: 46

34 II Corinthians 3: 13-15

35 Matthew 22: 36-40; Mark 12: 28-30

36 Matthew 5: 48 The word for merciful in the text is *oiktirmos*. The word for perfect is *teleos*, the same word used in the Definition from the Council of Chalcedon to describe the union of "perfect" man and "perfect" God in Christ.

37 Luke 6: 36

38 Matthew 22: 37; Mark 12: 30; Luke 10: 27. Mark and Luke add "strength" to the three other qualities from Matthew.

39 John 13: 34; See also John 15: 12

40 I Corinthians 11: 1

did interpret the law and express new requirements for righteousness, it was by his example and in his parables that the meaning of "love" and "neighbor" as well as "God" was understood. This was especially evident in the parable of the Good Samaritan, which was told explicitly to answer the question, "Who is my neighbor?"[41]

Even before Jesus, however, the Hebrew prophets had reinterpreted and expanded the Abrahamic understanding of imitating divine righteousness beyond the Mosaic code. Until I entered seminary, my knowledge of the Hebrew prophets was limited to names and dislocated quotations of wisdom, piety, and foretelling. A glimmer of insight during my college years into their concern with social issues beyond personal purity, as I became involved in the Civil Rights Movement, expanded during seminary to a passion for social justice. Amos, Hosea, Micah, Isaiah, and Jeremiah principally opened my eyes to Jesus' teaching about and care for the poor, the excluded, and the marginalized people of the world.

I began to understand the prophetic preparation for the Messiah in the Hebrew scriptures as a fulfillment of perfect and complete humanity and as an anticipation of one who would bear an unclouded divine message and presence rather than as a prediction of specific events. The prophets inferred from their own past and present experiences what the perfect human being bearing God's image, *i.e.*, the Messiah, would be like. Their hope and vision for the future were not some mystical and magical flash of esoteric knowledge unrelated to history and human psychology. Jesus was the Messiah deeply longed for as the completion of the dreams and hopes for full humanity, better envisioned and articulated by the Hebrew prophets than by all the wise people of other cultures and religions who had also shared those longings. When Jesus appeared as the hoped-for and longed-for Messiah, he surprised those visions and expectations by expanding the understanding of full humanity and revealing an unanticipated perfection of being human. My childish conception of a seer-like prediction of the precise events of Jesus' life was happily demolished and replaced by a truly prophetic

---

41 Luke 10: 29-37

understanding of complete humanity fulfilled in Jesus as the Christ (Messiah).

During this same period in my life a parallel process of disillusionment and re-evaluation took place regarding my provincial civic heroes. History for a southern boy from rural Georgia reverberated around the heroic exploits of paragons such as Robert E. Lee and Jefferson Davis and the founding fathers, Washington, Jefferson, Madison, Franklin, and Adams, and grudgingly even Abraham Lincoln. As an American history major in college, I began to realize that these men were all flawed and imperfect. The national heroes who lived during my childhood and youth, such as Franklin Roosevelt, Dwight Eisenhower, John Kennedy, and Martin Luther King, Jr., were also exposed by my middle-age as flawed men with grievous faults and personal transgressions. The realization that all of them were not plaster saints of unblemished perfection, however, freed me to see the real greatness of their achievements and aspirations and ideals, much as I was freed to see the prophetic visions of fuller humanity in the Hebrew prophets by relinquishing a notion of their mystical predictive powers. Jesus thus became more sharply focused and deeply appreciated as the perfection and completion of humanity from the perspective of those who had longed for him before his appearing and of those who aspired to his example in later centuries.

Although Jesus is sometimes portrayed in the New Testament as the new lawgiver in a recapitulated perfection of Moses,[42] I tend to see Paul and Moses in a closer parallel as lawgivers and ironically also as those who struggled for revolutions in human freedom. Moses led the Hebrew people out of slavery in Egypt, and the focus of Paul's ministry was the inclusion of the Gentiles in the promises of the divine covenant. Yet, Moses (at least in tradition) prescribed statutes on the most minute issues from ritual sacrifice to labor relations and property rights; and Paul gave instructions, for instance, about who could speak in church, what women should wear, domestic relations and sexual mores. In the same passage where Paul refers to the Mosaic law as "the ministry of

---

42 See references to the Gospel of Matthew above.

death, chiseled in letters on stone tablets," he writes that "where the spirit of the Lord is, there is freedom";[43] but two chapters later he is railing about lawlessness, licentiousness, and impurity.[44] Although the relationship between law and freedom in biblical faith is often polar, it is also sometimes overlapping and is always in tension.

If the parallel to Moses seems more appropriate for Paul than for Jesus in terms of the human tension between law and freedom, the parallel between David would seem apt for Jesus in the distinguishing aspect of Abrahamic faith that recognizes a divine presence that can be personally known and experienced and actually encountered and engaged. To be sure, the intimacy between Moses and God is noted in Exodus: " . . . the Lord used to speak to Moses face to face, as one speaks to a friend"; and indeed God told Moses that "I know you by name";[45] but what was said in these conversations was not revealed. Not until David and the later prophets, especially Jeremiah, are we privy to the dialogue between the Lord and a human person. It is more than as a category of genetic ancestry that the first verse of the New Testament, as noted earlier, refers to Jesus as the son of David and son of Abraham. The only identification of Jesus that precedes his lineage from David (who is listed first), and Abraham is his Messiahship. The breakthrough in human consciousness represented by Abraham of a personally known and experienced deity was "fleshed out" by David. Although the origin of many of the psalms traditionally attributed to David may be questioned by scholars much as the specific laws attributed to Moses are suspect, David represents the development of the "God-consciousness" that characterized Abrahamic faith much as Moses represents the requirement to imitate divine righteousness. In addition to his association with the psalms David also serves as a precursor for the Messiah in his God-consciousness in part due to the fullness and richness of his biography in the chapters from I Samuel

---

43 II Corinthians 4: 7 & 17

44 II Corinthians 6. Being set free from the curse of the law as death will be pondered at greater length in the final section on the "self."

45 Exodus 33: 11-12

16 through I Kings 2, which may have been written contemporane-
ously to his life.

More than half of the psalms are attributed to David in the King
James Version of the Bible, although some of them were written in a
later period of Hebrew history as evidenced by references detected in
a simple reading of the text without any literary or textual scholarship.
Yet, it is important to biblical piety that these psalms convey the spirit of
David's devotional faith, as the laws of the Pentateuch carry the spirit of
Moses' obedient elaboration of the covenant. The full title of the Book
of Common Prayer, even in its 1976 American revision, remains "The
Book of Common Prayer and Administration of the Sacraments and
Other Rites together with The Psalter *or Psalms of David.*" Once again
David is recognized at least symbolically as the author of the Psalter
and thereby the biblical prototype for a piety that represents person-
ally knowing and experiencing God and being actively encountered
and engaged by God.

The intimacy of David's relationship with God reveals his humanity in his contrition when confronted by Nathan over his adultery
with Bathsheba and complicity in Uriah's death and his grief over the
death of the child born of his immoral union with Bathsheba[46] as well
as his grief over his son Absalom, despite Absalom's betrayals, [47] and
over Saul and Jonathan, despite Saul's attempts on his life,[48] and in his
exuberant "leaping and dancing before the Lord" when the ark was
recovered.[49] The winsomeness of David's humanity is shown in the
depth of the love and loyalty he shows for Jonathan, Abigail, Michal,
and Bathsheba and the love and loyalty they returned to him[50] as well
as in the notable incident of the young soldiers risking their lives to
procure a draft of water from the well in his hometown of Bethlehem

---

46  II Samuel 12
47  II Samuel 19: 14
48  II Samuel 1: 17
49  II Samuel 6: 16
50  I Samuel 19 & 20

for which he had expressed a whimsical longing.[51] Yet, it is in the Psalter that we find the fullness of that aspect of humanity involved in an intimate "God-consciousness." Both in the psalms which David may have penned and in others attributed to him we find the personal experience and knowledge and encounter and engagement with God that David represents.

The conversation between the human soul and God from meditations in the Psalter will be further explored in later sections of this book on "Nature" and "the Self"; but the range of emotions can be sampled from a selection of the first verses of many psalms addressing God: "Lord, do not rebuke me in your anger; do not punish me in your wrath; have pity on me, Lord, for I am weak; heal me Lord, for my bones are racked" (6: 1-2); " . . . O Lord, will you forget me forever?" (13: 1); "I love you, O Lord, my strength" (18:1); "to you, O Lord, I lift up my soul; my God I put my trust in you, let me not be humiliated" (25: 1); "in you, O Lord, I have taken refuge; let me never be put to shame" (31: 1); "have mercy on me, O God, according to you loving kindness; in your great compassion blot out my offenses" (51: 1);[52] "hear my prayer, O God; do not hide yourself from my petition; listen to me and answer me; I have no peace because of my cares" (55: 1-2); "have mercy" (56: 1); "rescue me" (59: 1); "hear my cry" (61:1); "hear my voice when I complain" (64: 1); "save me, O God" (69: 1); "O God, do not be silent" (83: 1); "bow down your ear, O Lord, and answer me, for I am poor and in misery" (86: 1); O Lord, my God, my Savior, by day and night I cry to you; let my prayer enter into your presence; incline your ear to my lamentation, for I am full of trouble; my life is at the brink of the grave" (88: 1-3); "Lord, hear my prayer, and let my cry come before you" (102: 1); "Lord, hear my voice: if you, Lord were to note what is done amiss, O Lord, who could stand?" (130: 1-2); "O Lord, I am not proud" (131: 1); "Lord, remember David and all the hardships he endured" (132: 1); "Lord, you have searched me out and known me, you know my sitting down and my rising up; you discern my thoughts from afar,

51 II Samuel 23: 14-17
52 Psalms 51 and 139 will be pondered more fully in the final section on the "self."

... how deep I find your thoughts, O God! how great is the sum of them" (139: 1 and 16);[53] "deliver me, O God, from evildoers" (140: 1); "O Lord, I call to you; come to me quickly; hear my voice when I cry to you" (141: 1); "Lord, hear my prayer, and in your faithfulness heed my supplications; answer me in your righteousness" (143: 1). Jesus, who fulfilled a perfect God-consciousness in his intimate relationship with the Father, quoted two of the psalms attributed to David from the Cross: "My God, my God, why have you forsaken me?" and "into your hands I commend my spirit." (22: 1 and 31: 5)

Jesus commanded us in Luke's version of the Sermon on the Mount to be merciful as our heavenly Father is merciful;[54] and in Matthew's version of the Beatitudes, Jesus taught that the merciful are blessed, for they will receive mercy.[55] The evangelists note Jesus' compassion for the crowds and especially for the sick and the bereaved and demon possessed,[56] and Jesus blessed the example of mercy and compassion in the parables of the Good Samaritan and Prodigal Son and unforgiving overseer.[57] Yet, the more remarkable quality of mercy and compassion was evidenced by those who recognized it in Jesus himself over and over again and cried out to him to "have mercy on me."[58] Before the final days of his passion and crucifixion Jesus exhibited the fullness and completeness of perfect humanity most poignantly in his expression of compassion and mercy. In the way he expressed compassion Jesus was able to preserve the dignity of those to whom he had shown mercy without denying their humanity with a denigrating kind of pity.

In Hebrew scripture mercy *(chesed)* is usually thought of as a gift of God to people and is not often associated with human relationships. Compassion, closely akin to mercy was also a quality usually associated with God in the Hebrew scriptures, rather than a category

---

53 See note above regarding Psalms 51 and 139.

54 Luke 6:36

55 Matthew 5: 7

56 Matthew 9: 36; 14: 14; 15: 32; Mark 5: 19; 6: 34; 8: 2 Luke 7: 13

57 Luke 10: 33 & 37; Matthew 18: 33

58 Matthew 9: 27; 15: 22; 17: 15; 20: 30-31; Mark 5: 19; 10: 47-48; Luke 17: 13; 18: 38-39

characterizing behavior between human people. In some exceptional instances, Solomon is enjoined by God to show compassion on his people,[59] and Zechariah counsels during the exile that people should show kindness and mercy *(chesed)* to one another;[60] Hosea notes the lack of mercy *(chesed)* among the people of the land and writes that God desires mercy *(chesed)* and not sacrifice;[61] Micah similarly says that the Lord requires us to do justice and love mercy *(chesed)* in walking humbly with God;[62] and Isaiah notes the mercy (more in the sense of pity) that a mother has for a nursing child.[63]

As the Hebrew prophets expanded and deepened the law of Moses, so the prophets amplified the divine-human conversation in addition to their occasional references to imitating divine mercy and compassion. Isaiah and Hosea among others exhibited an intimacy with God that anticipated the perfect intimacy of the Christ with the Father; but it was Jeremiah who furthered the God-consciousness beyond David most markedly for me, in part due to his quarrelsome and candid arguments with God.

Perhaps because I was engaged during seminary in a semester-long exegetical seminar focusing on the book of Jeremiah, I regard him more than the other Hebrew prophets as the best precursor, though flawed, for the humanity of Jesus. Jeremiah's lament to God in chapter 20, when he accused God of tricking him and bringing mockery and derision on him and finally cursed the day when he was born, anticipates in some ways Jesus' prayer in the Garden of Gethsemene to let the cup pass from him.[64] Both went on to fulfill their calling and vocation, although Jesus showed graceful obedience and humility as well as perfection of purpose and will. Yet, in Jeremiah's conversations with God we see something of the intimacy with the Father that Jesus

---

59 II Kings 8: 50
60 Zechariah 7: 9
61 Hosea 4: 1; 6: 6; *Chesed* is also often translated as "steadfast love" or "kindness."
62 Micah 6: 8
63 Isaiah 49: 15
64 Matthew 26: 39

enjoyed. In buying the field in Anathoth even as the Chadaean army was overrunning the country, Jeremiah exhibited some of the hope for the future and trust in God that Jesus showed in their fullness and perfection as he faced his death.[65] In his Lamentations Jeremiah echoes and surpasses Moses who interceded for the people more than for his own safety and welfare and once again anticipates the intercession of Jesus for the human race.

As some of the heroes from the Old Testament anticipate the perfection of humanity in the Messiah, the saints of church history echo aspects of the humanity completed and fulfilled in Jesus. Many of the church fathers are studied for their doctrinal formulas rather than for the example of their lives. Martyrs follow the example of faithfulness even unto death and recall Jesus' sacrifice on the cross. In his *Confessions* Augustine eloquently expresses his search and journey toward full humanity. Perhaps for more people than any other figure Francis of Assisi serves as an exemplary imitation of Christ in devotion. So great was the identification of Francis with Jesus that the wounds from the cross appeared on his body.

More than any other period from the history of the Christian Church, however, the Celtic saints have influenced my perspective regarding the full and perfect humanity manifested in Jesus. As I prepared for retirement and during the first several years as a retired priest, I made five trips to Europe and studied in four courses focused on the Celtic Christian leaders from the fifth through the seventh centuries. Aidan is probably my favorite figure from church history after the biblical period. Like Jesus Aidan did not leave anything written by himself, and unlike Jesus only one short prayer was quoted by his disciples. His example of humility—he refused to ride a horse because he did not want to be above walkers—and generosity—he gave away every bottle of wine and a fine horse given to him—and perseverance—his patience with the wild heathen of Northumbria after others despaired of them—and concern for young people—his school at Lindisfarne that groomed the men who would convert much of England to Christian-

---

65 Jeremiah 32: 1-8

ity—all imitate the example of Jesus, who did not count equality with God something to be grasped and fed the multitudes and suffered the obtuseness of his twelve disciples and enjoyed a beloved relationship with John and prepared the apostles for mission.

Before Aidan, Patrick is credited with converting a nation to Christianity. Even though some of the exploits of Patrick, like those of other Celtic saints, may be exaggerated to myths and legends, his genius for accepting what was good in the pagan culture and society and transfiguring them by Christian grace affirmed the basic goodness of humanity to be redeemed and perfected by Christ. Patrick's desire to return and minister to the people who had kidnapped him at 16 and enslaved him for six years also reflected the incarnational example of the Son who came into the sinful world not to condemn but to save.[66]

In my visits to sacred Celtic sites I have gained new appreciations of the humanity which stretches toward fullness and perfection in Cuthbert, David of Wales, Mungo, Columba, Ebba, Kevin, Pelagius, Brigid, and others. One of the glories of Celtic Christianity was the equality and authority of women in the church. The most notable for me personally was Hilda, the great abbess of Whitby, who gave up some of her authority and risked her role so that Christians might find greater unity. Wilfrid was associated with Hilda, because of the Synod held at Whitby, and was perhaps the most maligned, along with Pelagius, of the Celtic saints. If Aidan mirrored Jesus, Wilfrid mirrored Paul, often exiled, shipwrecked, and denounced, but ever traveling and organizing efforts to convert lands, even those where he landed by misfortune.

All of these Celtic saints illustrated for me fragments and aspects of humanity striving toward the fullness and perfection found in Jesus and so illuminating those aspects of his true and complete humanity. Many other periods and characters from history might have been chosen to reflect facets of the humanity completed in Jesus, but I shall close this section with a brief survey of notable people in non-biblical religions that have expanded my understanding of what it means to be

---

66 John 3: 17

human. Closely related to Judaism and Christianity, Islam, the "other" Abrahamic faith, and its great prophet, Mohammed, testify to the supreme power of the one and only God. Although Jesus repeats the Jewish Shema, "Hear, O Israel: the Lord our God, the Lord is one,"[67] and taught that no one is good but God alone[68] and that "you have one Father—the one in heaven,"[69] he did not reiterate a belief in the omnipotence and oneness of God as often as did Mohammed; Jesus' emphasis was more on his intimacy and unity with the Father, especially as reflected in the Gospel of John. Although Jesus may be admired informally by modern Jewish rabbis, he is explicitly revered in the Koran. The Muslim interpretation of his life varies from the Christian story, but Christians should not forget how deeply honored Jesus is in Islam and how Mohammed witnesses to the absolute oneness and power of God as well as the marvelous attributes of God[70] that Jesus reveals in his teaching and example. The fidelity to the one, true God by my colleague Imam William Abdullah and by many Muslim friends who follow the teachings and example of Mohammed has illuminated the faithfulness of Jesus to the Father for me, and the hospitality of Muslims in my study and travel in the Near East as well as in the United States has exemplified the gracious welcome in Jesus' character more fully than that of most Christian strangers of casual acquaintance.

In my college and seminary study, the character of Confucius and his followers helped to focus the importance of respect and propriety in the human community and an ordered priority of values, which were dominant themes of Jesus' parables. The Hindu religion held less interest for me than other world religions, although some of the same gracious hospitality from Indian friends that I had experienced from Muslims (and often found lacking in Christians) echoed Jesus' kindness to visitors. Hinduism as well as the Taoist tradition of Lao-tze also emphasized the unity of human life with all living beings, which

67 Mark 12: 29; Deuteronomy 6: 4
68 Matthew 19: 17; Mark 10: 18; Luke 18: 19
69 Matthew 23: 9
70 For example, the 100 sacred names of Allah

is often sorely neglected in Christian history and tradition (and will be discussed more fully in the next section on Nature).

The unity of all earthly life has been most powerfully conveyed to me, however, through Buddhism and the life of the Buddha. For a few weeks in seminary, with the friendship and influence of a Buddhist monk, I attempted to live according to the principles of Buddhist practice and faith. I could not pretend even then to be a Buddhist because I could not accept the cosmology and metaphysics of that religion, especially the belief in the unreality and "evil" of the material world, which my incarnational faith regarded as potentially "God-absorbant." Even so, the compassion of the Buddha reflected for me the compassion of Jesus in a fuller way than any of the great heroes of the Old Testament and rivaled the saints such as Francis of Assisi and Aidan, who imitated Jesus' example of compassionate humility.

Buddhism is the only religion that ever tempted my allegiance outside the Christian tradition, and I have learned much about myself through meditation (to be discussed further in the section of "self") as well as the unity of all life and compassion from Buddhism and the Buddha. It would seem appropriate to conclude this section with Buddhism, which suggests a transitional anticipation of clues to the humanity of Jesus found in Nature and in myself, which will follow in the next two sections of this book. Buddhism is probably the highest expression in world history of humanism and thus illuminates for all religious traditions what it means to be human. It may not be possible to be a Buddhist-Christian or a Christian-Buddhist given the contradictions of their ontologies, but the compassion exemplified in the Buddha is an essential ingredient of true humanity; and so, for me, Buddhism and the Buddha disclose in a profound way aspects of the true humanity perfected and fully completed in Jesus.

# Autobiographical Vignettes II

During World War II Daddy found work in a nearby town when there was no appropriate job available in Canton. He stayed in a boarding house in Cumming from Monday through Friday because rationed gasoline was not available for travel except on the weekend. On Friday afternoons I would press my nose against the cold glass of the living room window hoping to see his car turn into the driveway. On weekday afternoons as I listened to soap operas with Granny on the radio I would look out her upstairs bedroom window from which the main road was visible, hoping that someone interesting and exciting would come to visit us.

Sometimes at night Granny would let me cuddle beside her in the high five poster bed where generations of my family had slept and some had been born. Granny was my home base of security and comfort, and I was her shadow as she pushed back the barn door like the men and wrung the chicken's necks for frying and churned milk for butter and whipped egg whites with a whisk in one hand and a big stone platter balanced and tilted on the other hand. Lemon pie was both my and her favorite desert. "One of these days I'm going to make a pie just for you and me to eat, every crumb ourselves with nobody else getting any." Alas, she never made good on that promise. She told wonderful stories about long dead relatives and could imitate anyone's voice and accent; but I was perplexed and troubled that she was too shy to speak in the company of other people at church and almost cowered before strangers and locally respected visitors to our home.

❧

Aunt Alma (called Almer by her siblings in their Appalachian *drawl), my grandmother's youngest sister, was married to a country doctor. Perhaps because they were more affluent than other relatives, our Sunday afternoon visits to the Pettit home often included dinner, a rare occurrence in visiting the other Quarles uncles and aunts. When my father graduated from college during the Great Depression and could find no work in his field, Uncle Doc gave him a job as a bookkeeper for his medical practice.*

*Aunt Alma was the greatest teaser of the Quarles clan, all of whom excelled in teasing; and when we were young teenagers she mercilessly inquired about our romantic crushes and seemed to know exactly whom we were "sparin'" and "spoonin'". She made the best watermelon rind pickles and pear preserves I've ever tasted.*

*Like many of the Quarles women she lived to an advanced age uncommon for her generation. Even after I was in college and seminary and serving congregations, I always dropped in to see her when I was back in Canton for a visit. Well into her nineties, many years after Uncle Doc had died, following several falls and breaks to her hips, I found her in the kitchen one hot July day—she never had air-conditioning—leaning on her walker and stirring a huge steaming pot on her range and sweating profusely. "Aunt Alma, what in the world are you doing?"*

*"I'm making them there pear preserves you like so much." The tree in her back yard produced hard pears that, as she often said, "weren't fittin' to eat" but made the best preserves in the world.*

*"Aunt Alma, you really don't have to do that."*

*"I most certainly do. Who else do you think is gonna do it? I ain't about to let 'em go to waste."*

$\backsim$

*The greatest influence on my early academic life was Aunt Alice, my father's older sister. She held a doctorate in history and taught for most of her life at Meredith College in Raleigh, North Carolina. Her life work was a multi-volume history of the Blount family, which produced several governors of North Carolina and Tennessee in the colonial period and the early years of the republic; but her passion was her students. Aunt*

*Alice was pleased with those who followed her into academia; but her great pride was in the young women who went into professions, especially the law, inspired by her course in constitutional history. She said that women had been teachers for generations and centuries, but their emergence into other professions was new and exciting.*

*Aunt Alice often lectured at junior colleges around North Carolina. Her friends worried about a single, unmarried woman driving her old Plymouth coupe, that she dubbed "Don Pedro," late at night in remote areas and asked what she would do if she had a breakdown. She responded that she would cut and strip a willow stick and gently beat the motor, as she'd done to naughty children in secondary schools before she began teaching in college, because it would probably just be something loose. She never explained the mechanism of how beating the motor would tighten anything up, but apparently it had worked on at least one occasion.*

*One of her standard lectures on her road trips was on "the strange career of Jim Crow." She insisted that it was merely factual history, not propaganda; but after the News and Observer published an article about her lecture just as the Civil Rights Movement was gaining momentum, a bomb, according to her—at least a large firecracker—was exploded on the front stoop of her apartment. For two maiden ladies living alone together it was a terrifying night.*

*Several years before her planned retirement, when she was burning the midnight oil preparing her presidential address for the North Carolina Historical Society, she suffered a massive stoke. For several weeks she was hospitalized and underwent physical therapy for several months. I inherited Don Pedro that summer of 1963 during my Clinical Pastoral Education course at Dorothea Dix Hospital in Raleigh. Despite her slurred speech and considerable paralysis she returned to teach her fall senior seminar before she finally retired, demonstrating her great courage and the grace and compassion of Meredith College and the kindness and generosity of many friends and colleagues who transported and assisted her.*

◆

*My great grandmother, Clementine Evans Latimer, held court from her bed in her nineties. Although she never weighed over one hundred pounds in her life and was called "Tiny" by her family, she ruled her family with a quiet voice. She invited me to sit beside her on her bed and encouraged me with apparent rapt fascination to talk to her about the things that mattered to me. A little hooked cushion was platted by her tiny gnarled hands for the antique rocker that Aunt Rachel had given me; and the Victorian rose globed lamp from her parlor, now electrified, hangs over our dining room table today. When the family gathered around the pump organ to sing hymns, my Grandfather Latimer would cajole his mother from the adjoining room, "Sing tremolo, Mother"; and Great Grandmother Latimer would harmonize over the melody with a high pitched, thin, reedy obligato that sounded to a child's ears like the eerie call from a distant world.*

◆

*As my mother's mind began to fail and fade, she started cleaning out the house and throwing away accumulated articles. "If you want anything out of this house, you'd better get it now," my father warned during a summer visit. "You might be interested in your grandfather's bank records."*

*W. F. (Bill) Keith was a lifelong farmer, but he had also been one of the founders of the Etowah Bank and had studied in Cincinnati for a few weeks in the dawning twentieth century in order to fulfill his role as a bank trustee.*

*Inside his ledger, unknown to my father, was a greater treasure— notebooks from my great grandfather and my great great grandfather: my great grandfather's love poems and his financial account of the proceeds from the Georgia gold rush, and my great great grandfather's hand copied mathematics book with problems solved in pounds sterling, gilders, and francs as well as dollars before there was an established currency in the United States, and his record of conflicts between white settlers and Indians on the border of the Cherokee nation before the Cherokees were exiled from Georgia.*

*All of the folios were interesting to me, especially the account of how a large portion of our farm was financed; and all were donated to the Archives of the State of Georgia, where the adjudication of disputes between white settlers and Indians created the greatest interest. It was known that certain men had been deputized to hear such cases in Georgia, but no written record had previously surfaced. Mackey Anderson Keith's adventures in territory, which would later become his home, where no people of European ancestry were then living, made the earth that nourished my childhood seem both a strange foreign land and also my familiar abode.*

*My Great Great Uncle John Matthew Keith, for whom I was named (after my father), further whetted my curiosity about my ancestry as a member of the Keith family. As attested in my Great Great Grandfather Allen Keith's ledger, Uncle John's father together with his brothers had left their wives and children for several months in the 1830s to search for gold near Dahlonega during the "Georgia Gold Rush," in order to add acreage to the farm they had claimed from my Great Great Great Grandfather George Keith's purchase of an $18.00 ticket in the Gold Land Lottery of 1832. They soon discovered that they could make a greater profit by selling fatback, brandy, and pots and pans and by lending money to other prospectors than they could derive by panning for gold, although they did find a few nuggets.*

*Uncle John had been too young to accompany his father and brothers to Dahlonega in the 1830s—he was not born until 1832—but their stories inspired him to strike out for California in the even greater excitement of the "49ers" Gold Rush. Following family wisdom gained from the accounts of his siblings, he engaged in selling provisions to other prospectors. He used his profits from the California gold fields to invest in early oil explorations in the West and became a multimillionaire in San Francisco.*

*Among the few things I have left from my Keith ancestors today are the primitive gold scales that they used to weigh nuggets during the*

*Georgia Gold Rush in the 1830s and Uncle John's dog whistle and a stick pin made from a nugget he panned in California before he found explorations for oil more profitable than those for gold.*

∽

*In the early seventeenth century a woman of the Carter family clipped twigs from boxwoods in England and kept them moist during the long Atlantic sea crossing and rooted them in Virginia. Between the American Revolution and the War of 1812 those boxwoods in Virginia were clipped, and the twigs were brought to Georgia and rooted. For seven years another woman of the Carter family hauled pails of water over several miles from her rude cabin to keep the young plants alive at the spot where her family would build their permanent home.*

*When the Rockefellers were restoring Williamsburg, their British agent tried to buy the now towering boxwoods of the rare English variety for landscaping the historic town, but another woman of the Carter family refused his offer. When he argued that the house could use a coat of paint that could be purchased with the funds he tendered, Rilla's grandmother responded that he could return if she couldn't feed her children and she would reconsider. (He did succeed in courting and marrying one of Rilla's aunts.)*

*The wedding reception for Rilla and me was given among the ten foot high boxwoods. When it was necessary to sell the farm in Georgia after generations in the Carter family, we clipped twigs and rooted the boxwoods for our home in Opelika, Alabama, and transplanted them to our home in Montgomery. We are attempting to repeat the process for our retirement home in North Carolina.*

*One of the mantels in the Carters' first permanent home in Georgia was installed in our home in Opelika and removed and placed in our home in Montgomery. (Some years ago the Smithsonian Institute produced a photographic display of the mantels, including the two from the Carter home, made in that area of Georgia between the American Revolution and the War of 1812 by an itinerant craftsman.) We have said, not altogether factiously, that as we move to take a new parish cure, the selection of our home requires a fireplace that will fit the Carter mantel. It would not, however, fit our small retirement cottage; but it is happily installed in Lauren and Neill's home in Durham, North Carolina.*

*The continuity of generations is symbolized—almost sacramental-ized—by the physical things passed down through the centuries. When they are living things, such as our boxwoods, they carry particular meaning as we bequeath our spiritual inheritance to our children and grandchildren.*

∾

*Quite recently I received a telephone call from a young woman named Keith who had descended from the slaves on our farm. She wanted to learn more about the stories that had been passed down to her from her great grandfather, Walt Keith, about the large tract of land that my great grandfather, Allen Keith, had deeded to the freed slaves on the southern end of the farm after the Civil War. It was a very unusual action for a slave holder of that period. He had believed that they needed some means to support themselves, even though many of them continued to work on the farm for him.*

*For several generations many of them stayed in close touch with our family. When my father told me, as a junior high school student, I'd better start farming and earn some money if I expected to go to college, we called Walt Keith, who must have been in his seventies or eighties, to ask if he could help us gather corn in the afternoons in the fall after my classes began and my hours were limited. Walt told wonderful stories, like my grandmother's stories, about our families in the early days after Emancipation, as we threw the ears of corn into the trailer behind the tractor. Both white former slave owners and black former slaves faced extremely difficult economic conditions. Those who learned to live and work together survived and prevailed.*

*I met a few very old people who claimed to have actually been born into slavery. Old Marget (Margaret) lived in a clearing deep in the woods at the northern end of the farm. She apparently didn't want to reside in the Keith community about two miles to the south on the land that been deeded by my great grandfather. I held tight to Granny's hand on several occasions as we walked between the big trees to Old Marget's place. She wore gray raggedy clothes that she washed in a big black pot in her yard, and to my child's imagination, she looked like a scary witch; but before many minutes had passed, she had lured me into her lap and given me sweets she'd made from wild honey.*

*Several times when my grandmother fell ill, Old Marget appeared at our kitchen door, unsummoned and unnotified. "I come to kere after Miss Fannie."*

*"How'd you know Mama was sick, Marget?" My father would inquire.*

*"I jus' knows these things, Mista John. The spirits done tol' me Miss Fannie be ailin'."*

*There are no longer any members of my family named Keith in Cherokee County Georgia; but there are a number of black citizens there named Keith, related to us by history and generations of affection.*

∽

*Freshmen were not allowed to make the annual tours with the Duke Glee Club to Miami and New York City, but a mononucleosis epidemic swept the campus in 1957. When several upperclassmen dropped out at the last minute, two or three of us were offered the chance to board the bus. My parents met us in Atlanta before our first concert and whisked me off to Muses to purchase accessories for the used set of tails that I'd bought from an ailing senior (which almost fit me).*

*My roommate was a graduate student who had served for several years as an air force pilot and who knew as few other men in the glee club as I did. He protected me from the jibes of upperclassmen and guided me through the cocktail parties thrown for us by alumni groups at every stop—as a Baptist boy from Georgia, alcohol had never before passed my lips. We spent hours talking together on the long daily bus rides and in our rooms in the evening. He enjoyed giving me big brother advice, and I appreciated being able to confide in him without his showing any ridicule or hint of snide superiority.*

*On our free day we lay on towels side by side on a beach near Miami. The newspapers were filled with accounts of a U-2 spy plane being shot down in Russia and President Eisenhower's denials that the United States had any planned flights over Soviet territory—Gary Powers must have wandered off course due to bad weather or an instrument failure. Bob told me that U.S. spy planes flew over Soviet territory regularly on specific orders from the Pentagon. He himself had made such a flight. It shattered my belief that an American President would never lie to us and initiated my life long tutelage in the ambiguities of good and evil in the realm of international politics.*

∽

*A few months after I arrived in Nicaragua I was invited to a dinner at the Gran Hotel one Sunday evening. The presidential election campaign was in full swing, and a rally during the afternoon was planned by the opposition party in the plaza a block away from the hotel. All would be well according to the American Embassy, but the Nicaraguan friends I had made through my housemate, Floyd Avary, advised staying away from downtown Managua. I heeded the advice of the Nicaraguans.*

*A church member, whom I believed to be a CIA agent, later constructed events for me as we strolled through the city; communist guerillas had arrived in the country several days earlier from Guatemala and Colombia. Guns for their use were hidden inside the trailers filled with cotton at the height of the harvest season. The marksmen stationed themselves on rooftops along Avenida Roosevelt, the main thoroughfare in the central city, and fired into the crowd trapped on the narrow street between the national soldiers and the armed guards of the opposition. As each side fired at the other the crowd made up primarily of peasants, who had been trucked into the city for a festive outing, were mowed down by the hundreds. The purported purpose of the plan was to so destabilize the country that the election would be delayed. (As always in such occurrences, the government made a very low estimate of causalities, but even from my limited acquaintance I heard of enough deaths and injuries to multiply the official statistics by several factors.)*

*Trapped for over twenty-four hours were the dinner party guests inside the Gran Hotel, where the opposition candidate for president and his entourage had fled. Anastasio Somoza, then head of the army, brought in tanks and lowered their guns and threatened to raze the building to the ground. (His more level headed brother Luis, the former President, had died unexpectedly thus necessitating the election.) The papal nuncio intervened and negotiated a peace treaty. After they were freed, the foreigners, who had been lodged in the hotel, were taken into the homes of expatriates. The family of one of our church members had Siamese cats as pets and took in some German businessmen. The cats pounced onto the stomachs of the German visitors during the middle of the night, who were sleeping in the bedroom where the cats usually slept, and frightened the Germans more than the threat to their lives in the hotel.*

*Strangely the telephones, which usually went silent during national emergencies, remained functional. I drove my VW beetle to the home of a church member, who had a short wave radio. I called all our members and asked them for a brief message and telephone number for family members in the United States whom we could contact through a phone patch to let them know that they were safe.*

*During the afternoon when I drove to Dave Stine's home in the hills, not far from my house, the roads were clear. Late that night as I sped home nervously, I almost collided with a roadblock set up by the Nicaraguan national guard. I was pulled from the car, thrown to the ground, frisked, and tossed over the bonnet of the VW. I was asked, in Spanish of course, for my official papers, my residence visa and permission form for owning and operating an automobile in the country (which was different from a driver's license). I realized that I had left them at home in my haste to get to Dave's house during the afternoon. I thought those soldiers were probably illiterate, so I pulled out my Durham, North Carolina, Ministerial Association card, which was elegantly printed with fancy calligraphy. The soldier said in English, "Señor, I both read and speak English." I thought I would surely be shot on the spot; but when he learned that I was the pastor of the Union Church, whose members included five ambassadors to Nicaragua, he let me go with a stern warning.*

*The next morning a Nicaraguan friend, whose husband was out of the country with Floyd on business, called me weeping from her home in the central city. A man had just been shot on the street and fallen against her front door, as the "mop up" operation continued by the national guard. I could do nothing except listen and pray with her. Then I went out on our back patio. I could hear the gunfire echoing across the volcanic lagoon that acted like a megaphone between our house and the city. The bees and hummingbirds were busy among the hibiscus. I felt the contrast between the violence of human affairs and the serenity of nature, and my location in an idyllic garden seemed almost surreal.*

ꙮ

*The first Episcopal Church I served in the United States after returning from my missionary stint in Nicaragua and sojourn in France was St. Wilfrid's in Marion, Alabama. Although there are numerous churches named for St. Wilfrid in England, especially Roman Catholic churches, I believe the only other Episcopal church in the United States named for the first Archbishop of York is located in California. Although I made several halfhearted attempts to learn about St. Wilfrid during my cure in Marion, I began to delve seriously into his biography years later; and I am especially grateful to him for leading me into a decade long exploration of Celtic Christian spirituality.*

*Wilfrid is much maligned in the Anglican circles of Britain and America and hardly acknowledged in the magnificent York Minster. His most evocative artifacts are the only two Saxon crypts left in England, both built by Wilfrid at Rippon Cathedral and Hexham Abbey, as well as his stone bishop's throne at Hexham. Although he is blamed for "doing in" the Celtic church by his role arguing for the Roman and Benedictine positions at the Synod of Whitby in A.D. 664, I would maintain that he preserved much of the Celtic tradition in the face of the inevitable emerging Roman and Benedictine hegemony. His concern was centered in the unity of the Catholic Church and the territorial integrity and authority of bishops. The other issues at Whitby were related to those principal is-*

sues. The date of Easter was germane to the unity of the church, and the matter of haircuts (tonsures), which seems silly to us today, symbolized whether monasteries would be pacifist under the authority of a bishop or armed militias ruled by a marshall abbot.

Unlike his spiritual alter ego, Cuthbert, whose stepmother was his greatest defender and confidant throughout his life, Wilfrid was ill treated by a cruel stepmother; but he found support as a teenager by appealing to a princess. He was supported by powerful women throughout his life, often to his detriment, when the jealousy of the male members of their families was aroused leading to hostile action against him. His appeal to women may have resulted in part because he was probably the most intelligent and most handsome man of his generation in northern England, and his conflicts with powerful men may have been caused in part by his naiveté and incredulousness.

I cannot identify with Wilfrid's beauty, but I do share a certain intelligence sometimes combined with a lack of practical common sense. I also share some of Wilfrid's stubbornness and unwillingness to compromise with a touch of his occasional vanity. I laud his stoicism in the face of great suffering and his ability to turn a horrible situation and circumstance into the occasion for bringing about good. His exiles, shipwrecks, and refugee sanctuaries were all used for the conversion of his hosts. More than any other missionary Wilfrid may be credited with the tactical conversion (or re-conversion) of England. Many of his faults I recognize painfully in myself, and many of his virtues are those which I most admire and to which I aspire.

❧

The year after I retired my sister and her husband invited Rilla and me to accompany them on a trip to Ireland for Glen to seek out his ancestral roots. After Glen and Ann returned to the United States, Rilla and I stayed in Dublin for a course on Celtic Christianity and made some visits to Celtic Christian sites. I especially wanted to find the last place where St. Columba had lived before he left for Scotland. The Celtic monasteries of Columba's era were like armed fortresses, often warring with one another. It was not until the time of St. Wilfrid that monasteries became pacifist. When Columba copied a Gospel manuscript from another monastery without permission, it provoked just such an inter-monastic battle. Columba was so chagrined (or chastised in another version of the story) that he fled to one of the most remote areas of Ireland. Even that didn't prove enough of a self-imposed exile and so he later removed himself to Scotland. (The conversion of Scotland was thus initiated not so much from evangelistic fervor as out of political and personal circumstances.)

Before we left on our trip Rilla happened to mention to our veterinarian in Montgomery that I wanted to reach the site of Columba's last cell and chapel in Ireland. The Irish rarely go to Chomcille Stad north of Sligo on the coast; the tourists never go there. George Millis had made several trips to Ireland to hunt red deer; and he suggested that Francie White, who set up the hunts, might be able to help us. George wrote Francie, who met us in Sligo and graciously agreed to drive us to the village and guide us to the ruins.

When we inquired about directions in the village, we received rather vague answers but determined that the walk would be too far for Rilla. Francie, his ten year old son, and I set off. We asked for directions from people we met along the way and were told to follow certain hedgerows and stone walls. We walked and walked and climbed and climbed. Finally we encountered a shepherd driving his sheep. I couldn't understand a word he spoke, but Francie told me that he had described the most detailed landmarks we had thus far received for directions. We walked and walked and climbed and climbed some more. Breathless and exhausted I said, "Francie, I think that shepherd was 'pulling my leg'," (having a joke at the expense of an American tourist).

"John, shepherds rarely lie."

We followed his descriptions and at last came to a hill overlooking a cove. The walls of the cell were still partially erect, and Columba's stone bed was completely intact. The smaller stone circles identifying the foundations of the other monks' cells surrounded Columba's. The stones of the chapel had crumbled around the foundation, but the spring at *its center bubbled up and reinforced the theories of Christian Chapels being built over the site of pagan Celtic places of worship, especially at sacred groves and wells. The quest to reach Celtic sites was always a large part of the spiritual reward; but viewing the ruins of Columba's last cell and chapel in Ireland, despite the difficulty of the drive and trek, far exceeded the adventure.*

*A nasty looking plastic cup rested on a stone beside the spring, left by the local people who made the arduous journey to drink the healing water. I declined to use it. Francie and his son drank from it lustily. That night I was ill with a stomach cramp. Francie and his son reportedly had no ill effects. . . . so much for germ theory.*

❧

*Almost exactly thirty years after leaving Nice, Rilla and I returned to France for a visit. In 1971 the plan had been to raze the exquisite little gothic style American church and sell the very valuable property in order to erect one more ugly Bauhaus apartment building. The mayor of Nice had summoned me to his office and shaken his finger in my face and told me that we'd never take a centime of the money from the sale out of France. He would tie up the sale in legal suits from then on. (The American Church was featured on many tourist brochures targeted at people in the U.S. who might visit the South of France.) The Huguenot pastor had mentioned one morning, visiting with me in my study, that they needed to move from their present building, a converted Napole-onic grain market, because the noise, the acoustics, the traffic, and the parking at that location had become insufferable. "Why don't you buy the American Church?" I asked him.*

*"How much are your asking for it?"*

*"I'm not part of those negotiations—thirteen million dollars, I think, but I bet they'd take eleven."*

*"Oh, we could never afford that."*

*But in the middle of the night it occurred to me that the Huguenot property was also very valuable and didn't have the emotional and historical liabilities connected to the American Church. What would happen if we swapped properties? I called Bishop Browning the next morning and made that suggestion. I had nothing further to do with it; negotiations were thereafter in the hands of lawyers and church officers in New York, but that was in fact what transpired. I also lobbied for some of the proceeds from the sale to be used for mission work in Europe rather than to pay off debts in the United States. Until our return visit, I had not been aware that this second suggestion had also been followed.*

*Rilla and I were received like triumphal heroes—we might have gone back years before, if we'd only known! The Huguenots had removed the exquisite alabaster reredos and carved carrara marble altar to conform the chancel to their austere style of worship; the loss of some of its beauty and elegance made me sad and a little sick; but it was still used as a church by Christian people, and the stained glass windows glowed as brightly as ever. Our former parishioners, while not entirely happy about the turn of events, were also deeply grateful that it had not been razed and was still a place of Christian worship.*

*By this time I was deep into my Celtic study, and one of our former members told me that it was now possible to visit Lérins, the island where St. Patrick had prepared for ordination before he returned to Ireland. Bunty LePage was a lovely native of New Zealand who had married a Frenchman and lived for most of her adult life in Nice. She graciously offered to accompany me to Cannes and take the ferry to Lérins. On the dock she went into the ladies' rest room and I into the men's before we boarded the boat. I was out several minutes before she emerged and sat down on a bench. When she came out, she didn't see me; and I walked down the quay, "Bunty, Bunty, I'm over here." In those few minutes the backpack which I'd left on the bench was stolen, containing my passport, my umbrella, my guidebook, and a pair of opera glasses, the only gift I'd ever received from my Grandfather Latimer.*

*"Maybe you'd prefer to go straight on back to Nice after this catastrophe, John."*

*"No, indeed, we've come this far. I want to see St. Patrick's chapel. I'll deal with getting a new passport later"—a process that took a precious day away from our planned agenda in Paris but was easily accomplished*

*through the services of U.S. consular officers, some of whom remembered some of my former parishioners in Nice from thirty years before.*

*Praying in the chapel where St. Patrick had prayed sixteen centuries before me took my breath away. I could almost feel him praying with me in the communion of saints. Despite the theft it was one of the best days of my life.*

౷

*Even in college I had a particular interest in Buddhism from our survey course on world religions, but I had never met a living, practicing Buddhist. In order to satisfy one of the requirements for our comprehensive examinations most Harvard seminarians took several courses at the Center for World Religions across the street from the Divinity School. As I passed through the hall after a class a resident Buddhist monk from Thailand in a saffron robe pulled me into a room in order to talk. I have no idea why he chose me among all the students leaving the classroom, but I was flattered to be chosen by him. Our conversations often continued after my classes. I can't remember what we talked about—I'm almost certain it was not specifically about religion—but it reinforced my interest and fascination with Buddhism.*

*Besides the parables of Jesus and the stories from the Hebrew scriptures and the legends from the saints of Christian history, the stories out of the Buddhist tradition have offered me the most poignant hints about what it means to be human. I once read that somewhere in the sacred writings of Buddhism there is a story that closely parallels Jesus' parable of the prodigal son, although I have never been able to locate its citation. In both stories the prodigal asks that his share of what he will inherit be given to him immediately, and his father accedes to his request. In both the prodigal travels to a distant land and wastes his money in debauchery with false friends. In both he is reduced to destitution and humiliated by degrading tasks. In both the son returns to his father's home, but here the stories diverge from one another. In Jesus' parable the son is welcomed with unconditional love and restored at once and lavished with kindness and presents. In the Buddhist version, so I have been told, the son is gradually restored to his former position beginning as one of the humblest roles of servanthood (what the prodigal had actually planned to request in the Christian version) and then working himself into positions of greater and greater responsibility and trust until he finally receives again all the rights and privileges of sonship.*

*Both stories speak truthfully to aspects of what it means to be human. The Buddhist version is probably preferable as a guide for rearing a rebellious child and epitomizes the central Buddhist virtue of wise compassion. Jesus' parable implies that for Christianity the essence of the meaning of the universe is unmerited grace and unconditional love.*

# The Place of Humanity
# in Nature

*" . . . God is testing [human beings] to show that they are but ani-*
*mals. For the fate of humans and the fate of animals is the same;*
*as one dies, so dies the other. They all have the same breath, and*
*humans have no advantage over the animals." —* ECCLESIASTES
3: 18-19 (NRSV)

*"When I consider your heavens, the work of your fingers, the*
*moon and the stars you have set in their courses, what is man*
*that you should be mindful of him? You have made him but little*
*lower than the angels; you adorn him with glory and honor; you*
*give him mastery over the works of your hands; you put all things*
*under his feet: all sheep and oxen; even the wild beasts of the field,*
*the birds of the air, the fish of the sea, and whatsoever walks in*
*the paths of the sea." —* PSALM 8: 5A, 6-9 (BOOK OF COMMON
PRAYER VERSION)

The relation of human beings to the rest of the created order
and their situation within the natural world present a para-
doxical tension as reflected in the contradictions expressed by
the Preacher of Ecclesiastes and the Psalmist. In this section we will
try to discern those aspects of our humanity that are revealed by our
place in Nature.

Jesus and all the other people of biblical eras were much closer to
the natural world than are most modern people in developed nations
today. Even during my own childhood, I had almost daily contact with

wild plants and animals in their natural settings, while as an older adult my daily experience of Nature involves primarily domesticated plants and pets.

From my earliest years I remember walking in fields and orchards with my father, who was an agronomist and who enjoyed describing how plants germinate and grow and mature. Farm animals and pets were always close by—cows, pigs, ponies, horses and mules, rabbits, guinea fowl, geese and chickens, dogs and cats, and goldfish. Wild creatures were adopted from a few days to several months, often to recuperate from injuries—turtles and tortoises, squirrels, raccoons, foxes, various birds and even snakes. For almost a year I kept in our basement a flying squirrel that had fallen from its nest as a baby. It often perched on my shoulder and sometimes terrorized female visitors by leaping into their hair. As a toddler a black racer (snake) followed my mother and me around the yard like a puppy as we gathered the stones from the yard of our new house so that grass might be planted. All these animals seemed as ordinary as the people who surrounded me and oftentimes were more familiar and intimate than human beings. The closest companion of my preschool and early grade school years was my Shetland pony, Princess Kate, who was the confidant of all my secrets and complaints. Later our border collie, Inky, served a similar role.

Jesus also drew from his experiences in an agricultural society to describe the meaning of humanity and express universal wisdom with metaphors from farming. Sowing and reaping grain, tending vineyards, cursing barren fig trees, planting and harvesting, pruning and fertilizing, seasons of rain and drought, of plenty and famine, observing foxes, lilies, thorns and brambles, swine, donkeys, and oxen permeated Jesus' parables to describe human nature and relationships to other people and to God. Jesus drew especially on the shepherd image from the Hebrew scriptures to describe the relationship between human beings and God, and sheep predominated in the metaphors and parables of Jesus and commanded the descriptions about Jesus by the Evangelists.

Yet, for me as also perhaps for Jesus, the awe and wonder of being a part and parcel of something larger than one's body, of being connected to something grander than one's immediate surroundings was experienced alone, in the wilderness, for Jesus often in the desert, for me in the Appalachian woodlands. The Evangelists all refer to Jesus withdrawing to lonely places, often to pray. When the wooded Georgia hills are filled with the fragrant pink and red and orange blossoms of native azaleas and the white elegance of the dogwood trees in the spring, when the whirring flight of quail are startling at footfall from a fallow field in the summer, when the leaves of hardwood trees blaze across the mountains and the aroma of ripening muscadines mingles with the scent of pines in the autumn, a sense of divine presence becomes imminent.

Although the presence of the Risen Christ is always promised to believers and sometimes felt in the Eucharist during Christian worship in the church, there is another sense in which those who have followed and studied the life of Jesus may feel that they are where he was when sitting beside a rushing stream or lying on the sand of a beach at sunset and that in those moments he is where we are. The immediate experience of Nature conveys a sense of connection to a larger creation than our own bodies and hints of divinity beyond the limitations of words and rational perceptions. The psalms are replete with images of divinity through metaphors from Nature, and Jesus had a particular genius for applying them to human affairs—from God's care for us as God cares for the fallen sparrow to providing for our needs as God clothes the fields with lilies.

As a child my travels to relatives' homes even in neighboring states were largely confined to the plains and foothills and mountains of the Appalachian region, except for occasional weeks of family vacation at Pawley's Island on the South Carolina coast. Mountains and oceans throughout my life have uniquely led me away from petty concerns and egotistical preoccupations and obsessive worries with their momentary and current appearances toward a perspective of eternity and the ultimate goals of divine providence.

Jesus chose a mountain for the epiphany of his transfiguration, so that mountains must have had a significance for him, too.[1] Surely the choice of a mountain was both personal and intentional as the setting for his most mystical revelation before his resurrection. Although there are perhaps more references to the sea in the Gospels than to any other natural phenomenon, they are usually to the freshwater Sea of Galilee, more like a large lake, than to the ocean or Mediterranean Sea. Nevertheless, Jesus' frequent presence and many of his important actions related to large bodies of water included his walking on the beach and calling his disciples and crossing the waters in a boat and bringing forth fish from the depths and calming its storms.[2] As a mountain was chosen for his transfiguration, one of the cardinal appearances of the Risen Christ was beside the Sea of Galilee at daybreak.[3]

As I grew older and traveled more widely, other numinous settings in the natural world evoked glimpses into the mystery of the created order and intimations of a divine presence. The first airplane flight of my life to a conference in Canada, when I was a college student, afforded a side-trip to Niagara Falls and an awed reverence before that great cataract. During seminary I served in the National Parks ministry for a summer in Yosemite Valley and was able to climb to the lower part of Yosemite Falls almost every day to eat my sandwich lunch. I hiked in the high Sierras during my days off, and each night I contemplated the shadows of the massive granite cliffs of the valley in the moonlight. Not only my geographical but also my spiritual horizons were broadened in the experiences of mountains and waters higher and fuller than the beloved green hills and rushing brooks of Appalachia, (although the Appalachian mountains and streams would always be my seminal lodestones for experiencing the natural world).

Throughout my life I have returned to the mountains and the sea

---

1 Whether the Transfiguration took place on Mt. Tabor, as the tradition has asserted, or some other mountain, it was associated with a mountaintop in all three synoptic accounts: Matthew 17: 1-8; Mark 9: 2-8; Luke 9: 28-36

2 The so-called nature miracles will be discussed more fully below.

3 John, chapter 21

hoping to replicate or preserve an experience from the past, often like Peter after the transfiguration event, but finding instead new experiences and insights. Even though each experience in life is unique and fraught with the possibility of new insight, the ever changing moods and subtleties of Nature, even (perhaps especially) at the same venues, often evoke a fresh and refreshing understanding.

The five years I lived in Nicaragua expanded my consciousness of diversity and variety in the natural world and opened my mind and spirit to suggestions of yet more new realities. Although summer thunderstorms in the mountains can be frightening and ocean waves crashing against the rocks can demonstrate power, a different kind of power is elicited by seeing volcanic eruptions and feeling earthquakes, and a different kind of terror is evoked by hearing the cries of animals in the jungle and enduring sudden tropical storms and floods. New visions of beauty also emerge in the flamboyant colors of tropical birds and flowers. The same storms that begin suddenly also often cease suddenly leaving a quality of repose, and the terrifying cries in the jungle at night can be interposed with a dark velvety softness as moonlight reflects off palm fronds providing a balm to the human spirit.

The psalms are filled with the contrasts between the terrors and powers of Nature and the beauty and comfort of Nature. The power and majesty of God are pondered in the thundering heavens, in hailstones as the earth is shaken, and in seabeds that are laid bare by the wind. The accounts of Jesus calming storms at sea recall not only a sense of the power of the holy in Nature but also a new conception of his authority over the powers of Nature.[4]

A quarter of a century after leaving Nicaragua I began a study of the Celtic saints who gave expression to the feelings and images of Nature that had arisen in the jungles of Central America. Although the Celts of Europe witnessed manifestations of Nature's power and terror far different from the tropics, they were able to combine intimations of the awe of divine majesty with the beauty of holiness in their observations

---

4  These so-called nature miracles present some problems for modern empirical scientific reasoning that will be discussed below.

of the natural world. The presence of God was not perceived so much in rainbows and bluebirds and butterflies and manicured formal gardens as in lightning, wind, and fire. The beauty of the holy was suggested by the natural world, but an awe and reverence of God was evoked by the majesty and power and wildness of the Creation.

During my youth and in the intervening years between my residence in Nicaragua and my study of Celtic Christianity, the romantic approach of beauty and delight in Nature dominated my reflections on the implications of the holy in Creation, and that romantic sentiment continues to be an important element for me in relating the presence of God to the experiences of the natural world. Although an immediate experience of Nature has been important throughout my life, and I have been made aware of how my spirit has shriveled in its absence when I once again have direct contact with the natural world, I do not have a daily inner impulse or weekly compulsion to walk in the woods or dig in the garden. As boys after school each day my brother Tom could not wait to run into the woods to swing on vines and climb trees and splash in the creek. On most afternoons I was content to play the piano or read books or look at reproductions of great visual art.

Although music, poetry, and art cannot substitute for the immediate experience of Nature, they are for me mediators of a wider world in the interims between direct encounters in the outdoors. Even on my hikes and garden strolls, I am inclined to be contemplative and passive, again unlike my brother who is actively engaged and physically involved with the elements of Nature. It is hard to know whether Jesus was more inclined to contemplation or action, but we do know that he walked (of necessity) long distances in the countryside and observed many natural phenomena and engaged in fishing and sailing.

Perhaps art, music, and poetry should not be considered as categories of Nature; but even when they do not explicitly refer to the natural world, they have the effect on me of opening my consciousness and my spirit to a world and a reality beyond my personal concerns and individual perspectives. Music has always been especially important for breaking open the limits of my mundane cares and preoccupations and transporting me toward a sense of wider and fuller universal reality. As a child I would lie beside the piano as my mother played hymns and popular music and later beneath the grand piano of my teacher, as she played classical compositions; and I would enter another world in the way that much later in life I was overwhelmed by beauty and grandeur inside a great cathedral or before a masterpiece of visual art.

At many times I was able to play myself out of dark moods on the piano or sing myself into the rapturous joy of life. (It is possible that I have always had a special interest in birds in the wild, because their songs remind me that my own musical voice was the gateway to a world beyond my immediate confines.) If given the choice between hearing a live symphony orchestra and hiking to the brow of a mountain, I would probably usually have chosen the symphony; but if I neglect too long a direct contact with the beauty and power of Nature, my spirit begins to wither, however many cultural mediators may have intervened.

We have scant evidence that Jesus was greatly influenced by art and music. The only reference to his involvement with music in the Gospels is the hymn that was sung at the Last Supper.[5] Even though he often went to the Temple in Jerusalem, Jesus neither affirms not denies its beauty when others praise its adornment.[6] He was surely moved by the poetry of the psalms, which he often quoted and had probably memorized in great portions, and his own parables reflected the beauty of Nature with verbal poetry; but I have a suspicion that Jesus was more like my brother Tom than like me in his relationship to the created order. His experiences were probably direct and immediate and actively involved with natural phenomena, rather than often or dominantly mediated by artistic representations and surrogates.

If art sometimes functions as an interpreter and mediator of Nature for the human spirit, science serves as Nature's interpreter and expositor for the human mind. Especially today when the very viability of the natural world is threatened by human activity, it is incumbent on us to ponder rationally the role of humanity as part of Nature in addition to

5   Matthew 26: 30; Mark 14: 26
6   Luke 21: 5

sensing our place in the natural world romantically and feeling our part of the created order spiritually. The present age presents an irony in the contrast between the exponential increase in our understanding about the workings of Nature in recent decades as opposed to our behavior that has resulted in catastrophic damage to the fabric of the created order. My scientific study and knowledge have been very limited, but it is also incumbent on those of us who are untutored in the complexities of biology, chemistry, geology, and physics to discern the proper place and role of humankind in Creation. Ecological practices must rely on the particulars of environmental science; but ecological theology must also return urgently to the query of the psalmist, "What is man that you should be mindful of him?" with new and altered answers.

As a reasonably well-read person, although untutored in science, the debate about evolution is for me a theological issue. Although the theory of evolution makes more sense to me rationally than the theories of creationism or intelligent design, I do not have the factual knowledge to make an informed scientific judgment and argument. The theories of creationism and intelligent design as they are usually expounded, however, contradict my understanding of ultimate truth as focused in the life of Jesus, although certain aspects and interpretations of them might be included in a fuller expression of the place of human beings in the created order.

Jesus is our prototype illuminating the interplay between  divine freedom and power with human freedom and potency. If God determines every aspect of every outcome in Nature, then the freedom and potency of created things are nullified. Modern physicists have suggested the possibility of indeterminacy even in subatomic matter, which would imply a certain degree of freedom at the most basic level of Creation. Yet, the theory of creationism would seem to deny any such freedom even to human beings, the most developed members of the created order to our knowledge. Thus I am unable to accept the theory of creationism because it compromises the human freedom and potency revealed in Jesus' humanity. At the same time the theory of creationism serves to remind us of the truth that divine freedom and power are always dominant and may on occasions contravene human freedom and potency.

The theory of intelligent design is troubling—and reminiscent of deism—in obscuring God's involvement in the ongoing processes of Creation. Thus I am unable to accept the theory of intelligent design, as it is often expressed, because it compromises divine freedom and power as being involved in a continuing process. Yet, the theory of intelligent design serves to remind us of intricate patterns in the created order which hint at a divine Creator. No matter how intricate the patterns in the most developed organs, such as human eye and ear and brain, however, explanations of natural biological mutation, selection, and development can be convincing as possible causes of their origin.

The most compatible theory with my own personal faith would be some type of statement of evolution. Although natural selection might be a sufficient scientifically rational explanation for human development, the interplay between divine freedom and power with biological freedom and potency cannot be disproved. By faith we can affirm that God leads us and nudges us toward an outcome of divine ordination. Faith believes (but cannot prove) that this process reaches an apex and culmination in the interplay between divine freedom and power with human freedom and potency. Such a notion of sanctified evolution cannot be proved or even supported by scientific inquiry, but faith can be understood as compatible with such a theory of evolution carefully expressed. The mystery of the interplay between divine freedom and power with human freedom and potency posits a process which envisions the pinnacle of what it means to be human.

The relationship between human beings and the other parts of the created order raises the issues of human limitation and potency, mutual dependence and influence, order and unpredictability, and determinacy and freedom. In each of these polarities we find hints about what may be the relationship between human beings and God.

A part of being human is being aware of limits and limitations, and nowhere are limits and limitations more evident than in relation to the natural forces of the world. We are helpless to prevent the destruction of storms and earthquakes and floods, although we have the capacity to predict some of their onslaughts and to ameliorate some some of their consequences. We are equally unable to initiate the blessings of benign seasons and favorable harvests and good health, although we possess some capability for achieving beneficent influences in all these areas.

The incidents when Jesus seemed to defy the limitations of his humanity in the so-called nature miracles are for me very problematical and confusing. If Jesus was able to cross the borders that restrict human freedom at will, he would not seem to be subject to the tension between freedom and natural law that characterizes humanity. My problem with the so-called miracle stories in the Gospels does not arise so much due to their conflict with modern scientific theory as due to the compromise they imply to Jesus' full humanity. If Jesus simply looked like a man "veiled in flesh" as some sort of docetic avatar, then his humanity is so *sui generis* different from ours that the point of this book (and indeed much of classical Christian dogma) would seem to be fallacious.

The many healing accounts in the Gospels can be harmonized with an understanding of a fully human Jesus, because God can use human beings, then and now, as instruments of divine salvic power, especially in those attuned to divine presence, as Jesus was perfectly and purely. The stories about feeding the multitudes can similarly be understood as the employment of a divinely chosen human agent.[7] In both of these situations Jesus as fully God and fully man would have been both the divine designator and the human designee, but the limitations which characterize humanity would not be violated.

The narratives about Jesus walking on water and to a lesser extent those about his calming storms are much more troubling to me. I have sometimes rationalized the stories about Jesus walking on water by

---

7    In the multiplication of the loaves it should be noted that Jesus started with bread, not with stones, as in the narrative of his temptation. Thus the account of the loaves and fishes supports the generous provision of God by amplification, not by magic. All the miracle stories involving Jesus can be read as corrections to the false magic offered to him in the temptation narrative.

relating them to the experiences of many fishermen who spend their whole lives on the sea but never learn to swim. During my sabbatical study in Israel in 1996 I was told that many fishermen on the Sea of Galilee even today cannot swim, and I later learned that such a lack of ability to swim was not uncommon in other people who make their livings on the sea. It is not difficult to speculate that Jesus' disciples, even those who had been Galilean fishermen, might not have been able to swim or at best could tread water by "dog paddling." Further speculation might suppose that if they saw someone approaching them using a modern "crawl stroke," they might refer to it in awed fashion as "walking on water." Such rationalization is finally satisfying neither to the intellect nor to the heart, however; and I must leave the question of Jesus' nature miracles in the realm of unanswered mystery and in the limbo of paradox by affirming both the simple truth of the obvious reading of the scriptures and also the true humanity of Jesus.

In pondering the dependence of human beings on the other parts of Nature and the effect of human behavior on the natural world, we discover clues and metaphors for our dependence on God and the interplay of our freedom and potency with the *telos* of the divine intention for the universe. As in the other three sections of this book—our study of history, our encounter with other people, and (later) our meditation on our inner selves—the principal aim is the discernment of what it means to be human. The survey of our place within the network of Nature, how we are limited by being only a part of it and how we have an effect on all other parts, echoes the goal of discerning what it means to be human; but the exigencies of our time impel us toward another equally crucial goal: the discernment of how we define what it means to be human threatens or restores the health of the whole created order.

Once again I offer the caveat of scientific ignorance. I am unable to proffer scientific solutions to the threats of climate change or over-population or the exhaustion of natural resources. Other people who are trained and equipped with technical expertise will have to prescribe the specific steps of a process for us. Rather I shall close this section with some statement from the perspective of my personal faith and (as above) autobiographical experience.

Both in his teaching and in his patterns of behavior Jesus is the exemplar of living fully but simply in harmony with Nature. He taught us not to be anxious about life, what we eat and drink or what we wear.[8] After he left his parents' home he had no permanent dwelling. [9] Jesus' words and pattern of living simply were vividly impressed on my consciousness in Central America especially during my years residing in Nicaragua and in many trips to Honduras. The ability of people to survive with few resources and little income was impressive, but their dignity and joy and generosity were even more remarkable. For Jesus as for those people whose lives I shared in Central America, the petition from the Lord's Prayer to "give us this day our daily bread" was more than a pious sentiment, it was a plea born out of the circumstances of their actual existence. They did not know if they would have sufficient nourishment and shelter for that day, nevertheless whether tomorrow would afford sufficient food or resources to face the challenges of survival.

Yet, the followers of Jesus in Central America seemed far less anxious and far more joyful than the affluent members of churches I had known in the United States. Often material opulence seems to result in a joyless inner emptiness. Jesus and the people of Central America also seemed to enjoy the good things of the earth and were more inclined to sharing than to accumulating and hoarding. Jesus noted that he was accused of being a glutton and a drunkard, because he greatly enjoyed eating and drinking with other people.[10] The Pharisees who criticized Jesus' enjoyment of the material world represent the puritans in every age who deny the pleasures of the body and focus only on the soul. It is a false dichotomy that implies the heresy of denying the Incarnation: God's embodiment in the material world of flesh and life. In finding the meaning of our human place and role in Nature, we should recall

8   Matthew 6: 25ff
9   Matthew 8: 20; Luke 9: 58
10  Luke 7: 34

"the scholastic adage that 'grace does not destroy nature but perfects it.'"[11] Jesus introduced his ministry to the world at a wedding feast, which was the happiest occasion of the society in his time; and he often compared God's kingdom to the "biggest party in a village," the marriage celebration that often took place over a number of days.[12]

It would be a mistake, however, to over sentimentalize a life of poverty and scarcity. The joy of eating and drinking may partly result from their contrast with the anguish of hunger and thirst, but the pleasure of having hunger and basic needs satisfied is not an adequate compensation for the pain of physical deprivation. In his parables Jesus taught about the importance of conserving seed and yeast and flour and sheep and bread and wine and even a few coins[13] Some of the practices by which the poor people of the developing world eke out their existence are destructive to the environment and ultimately self-defeating for their own survival. Poor women in Central America seem to spend their lives gathering wood and hauling water from remote streams, and as forests are stripped and streams polluted and depleted the conditions for their lives are made even harsher and more desperate.

The freedom and anxiety and the joy and generosity demonstrated in Jesus' life and teachings and modeled for me by the poor Christians of Central America must be balanced by the lordship of Jesus in his authority and power over Nature. Several times in the preceding paragraphs of this section, I have touched on my ambivalence and confusion in understanding the "nature miracles" of Jesus: the multiplication of loaves and fishes, walking on water and calming storms at sea. The question arises in each of these stories about whether Jesus is acting out of his human nature or out of his divine nature; but even if they proceed from his divine nature, the integrity of his human nature cannot be violated, as noted above, without the collapse of the doctrine of the Incarnation and the nullification of his full and complete

11 Carol Zaleski, "Faith Matters: The Thing with Feathers," p. 35, *The Christian Century*, June 3 2008, vol. 125, no. 11
12 For example, Matthew 9:15, Mark 2: 19; Luke 5: 34; 12: 36; 14: 8)
13 See Matthew, chapter 13, and Luke, chapter 15

humanity as our model and example. While magic must be avoided in the relationship of Jesus' humanity to the other parts of the natural world, mystery cannot be evaded.

In the mystery of Jesus' authority and power in and over and through Nature we see the final (and perhaps most important) clue from our relationship and place in the created order to what it means to be human. Because we cannot explain how Jesus calmed the roiling waters of the sea, we are reminded that we cannot fully explain or understand the humanity of Jesus, nor certainly explain or understand his divinity and the Godhead, nor even completely explain or understand our own humanity. The psalmist ponders the mystery and power of the human creature as a manifestation of the mystery and power of all created life which in turn are indications of the mystery and power of God. "I praise you for I am fearfully and wonderfully made; wonderful are your works . . . . How weighty to me are your thoughts, O God! How vast is the sum of them!"[14]

The aspects of what it means to be human gleaned from Nature may save us from an idolatry of the second person of the Trinity. We can trivialize Jesus' humanity in and with us by overemphasizing "what a friend we have in Jesus" to the exclusion of his authority and mystery. Jesus came to be with us and for us as our brother and also as our lord, but not as our buddy or as our pal. Krister Stendahl expressed some implications of this temptation in his Harvard Divinity School Convocation address in September 1984. "My own feeling is that we have overdone anthropomorphism in the interest of I-Thou-ing ourselves through life and into eternity. And I take it we will be surprised. I take it that there is nothing wrong in also thinking about God in a dialectical way as Energy, Wisdom, Light, Justice . . . ."[15]

Thinking about God in more than relational and personal terms that are subject to psychological analyses may save us from attempting to put God into the box of our minds. If the idolatry of former generations was expressed by making divine images in wood and stone, our

---

14 Psalm 139: 14 & 17 (NRSV)

15 "To Speak About God," p. 9, *Harvard Divinity Bulletin*, vol. 36, no. 2

temptation is manifested by making idols in our minds and attempting to capture God in ideas and rational propositions.

To reverse the order of the psalmist: when the power and mystery of Nature remind us that we cannot fathom the mystery and power of God, we are led to the humility that we cannot exhaust the meaning of what it is to be human with the exclusively personal explanations of our relationships with other people or even with the lessons of human history. Nature serves to remind us not only of its own mystery and power and beyond itself of a divine mystery and power that transcend the reckoning of reason and logic but also to evoke the sense of mystery and potency in our own humanity that can never be fully comprehended or explained. Nature cautions us that we are part of a mystery and power greater than ourselves and that we play responsible roles in and for the sake of that mystery and power; and when it cannot be fully analyzed and explained (perhaps even because it cannot be fully analyzed and explained), Nature contributes large elements to our understanding of what it means to be human as part of something larger and greater than ourselves.

# AUTOBIOGRAPHICAL VIGNETTES III

*For a majority of the years of my life I have had a dog as a pet, from the Airedale when I was a toddler to the succession of four miniature or toy poodles in recent years with a Boxer and a mutt in Nicaragua in between; but Inky, the border collie pet of my youth, was the most beloved. Dogs try to communicate with you. They tell you what they want and need and try to understand what you demand in order to please you. They become upset when you are upset, and they share your exuberance. Their loyalty and affection are unparalleled. They even demonstrate some empathy for your sadness and pain, but not like horses.*

*Horses listen and can be examples to human beings in the skill of listening. Horses don't respond or criticize or advise; they just listen; and yet, they convey empathy perhaps more deeply than human beings or any other living creature. During the lonely years of my childhood I poured out my thoughts and feelings to Princess Kate, my Shetland pony, as I rode her over the dirt roads and forest trails and pastures on our farm.*

*Without any conversation or prior warning my parents decided that I was growing too large for Princess Kate and that I could ride one of the big farm horses. They took her away and sold her while I was at school one day, so that I would be spared the pain, so they thought, of seeing her leave; and consequently I never had a chance to say goodbye.*

*More than five decades later during a discussion at the Kanuga Conference Center, when we were sharing stories of former pets, I began to talk about Princess Kate; and I burst into tears. I understood for the first time why I have been resistant over the years to riding horses. At last I was able to express my grief and acknowledge the painful memory of a loss that had been deeper than any I would know for many years until the people I loved began to die.*

∽

*During the summer I enjoyed driving the tractor to the field and seeing the budding and blooming trees and plants and occasional small animals along the way. Driving the tractor up and down the rows of corn for the rest of the day was a tedious bore, and I tried to distract myself by singing operatic arias at the top of my lungs to drown out the motor.*

*During the winter I detested driving the tractor to the sorghum syrup mill in the morning before school. Sometimes the temperature was close to freezing; and despite gloves, toboggan, earmuffs, a scarf, and a heavy jacket I shivered in the cold wind. My compensation was seeing many small animals—rabbits, foxes, raccoons, 'possums—more visible without the cover of vegetation and more lethargic and moving more slowly in the cold of winter than in the heat of summer.*

*Just before Lauren married Neill she wanted to make a trip separately with her mother and her father. We chose to take a tour by snowmobile in Yellowstone where the budding professional photographer made wonderful shots of the park and the animals in the snow and ice. Her photographs were later featured at a one woman show at Auburn University Montgomery. The huge animals, hundreds of times larger than those I'd seen on the farm in Georgia were also lethargic and slow and more visible and approachable in the wild than they'd been on our summer trip to Yellowstone, but they still reminded me of my winter tractor rides to the sorghum syrup mill almost a half a century previously.*

∽

*Barbara Martin, the wife of my most faithful childhood friend, has made many trips to the Holy Land. She fervently believes that the Garden Tomb is the site of Jesus' resurrection. Historical evidence convinces me that the Church of the Holy Sepulcher houses the empty tomb. It is serendipitous when the spiritual testimony of history and Nature coincide, but just as often they may be contradictory.*

*The continuous jockeying for position by competing factions of Christians, sometimes even involving a physical struggle, at the tomb*

*in the Holy Sepulcher presents one of the most unsavory pictures of his-*
*torical tradition. During the month I studied at St. George's College in*
*Jerusalem I often strolled to the Garden Tomb and sat and meditated,*
*and like Barbara I felt the presence of the Risen Christ. Resurrection*
*life by very definition is not confined to the chronology and physical*
*limitation of earthly history.*

*The garden where I most often felt the presence of the Risen Christ,*
*however, was located at Grace Church in Mt. Meigs, Alabama, perhaps*
*because I walked among the flowers and shrubs there more on Easter*
*Days and also on other days of the year than anywhere else, but it was*
*at the altar at Grace Church where I received the real presence of the*
*Risen Christ most often, most fully.*

*We may become aware of the Risen Christ in any setting—and gar-*
*dens are especially felicitous venues—but in the sacraments grace and*
*faith are united, and the present and the past meet in a way that the*
*convergence of history and Nature can never quite achieve.*

∾

*As a boy wandering across the farm on my pony and on various*
*days and nights in Central America and at other times and places I*
*have thrilled at the beauty of the natural world and felt myself a small*
*part of the immensity of Nature; but my communion with Nature day*
*after day, night after night was experienced most consistently and con-*
*tinuously during the summer I spent in Yosemite Valley in 1962. Any*
*hours of daylight between my shifts at the desk of the Yosemite Lodge*
*involved hikes to one of the waterfalls in the valley. The tent I shared*
*with two roughneck California teenagers lacked electrical connections,*
*and we would slip out in the darkness to see the stars and watch the*
*moon cast shadows on the granite cliffs and fall asleep listening to the*
*gurgle of the Merced River.*

*If I had two or more days off, I would head out of the valley to hike*
*in the high Sierras. When I could find no one to accompany me, I de-*
*cided to climb Mt. Hoffman by myself. In the middle of July I stripped*
*off all my clothes and enjoyed a skinny dipping snow bath at the base*

*of the peak. My notorious confusion in reading maps almost led to my death, when I found myself on a ledge on the wrong trail without any equipment. Like a cat in a tree I couldn't move up or down. One wrong half-step and I would plunge down hundreds of feet. Below me the snow fields glistened in the sun. Around me the mountain peaks of the Sierras shimmered in blue mists. Above me the peak of Mt. Hoffman hovered in magisterial grandeur. And inside me the incredible beauty of Nature and the unspeakable terror of Nature were joined.*

∽

*For several decades my only musical endeavors have been singing and playing hymns and Bach chorales and rarely, only every few years of so, attempting to play a classical composition or sing an operatic aria that I had once mastered, only to prove to myself that I could no longer render them; but even the hymns and liturgical music sung in church and the chorales and hymns played on the piano at home sometimes have the power to transport me into a wider world, where I feel a small part of something larger and grander than myself.*

*The purest such moment of self-transcendence, however, was experienced when I sang the Fauré Requiem with the Choir at the Duke University Chapel. Voicing the music of "requiem eternal" I felt myself a member of the communion of saints throughout the expanse of the present world and from eras and generations of centuries past and perhaps unto ages yet to come, and even "with Angels and Archangels, and with all the company of heaven."\**

*\*(From the "Sanctus" in Holy Eucharist, The Book of Common Prayer, page 334)*

∽

*Green parrots mate for life. When I returned to Nicaragua for a visit a couple of years ago, I asked Jonathan to drive me to the Masaya Volcano so that I could see the pairs of parrots fly into their nests in the walls of the crater at dusk. Biologists have been unable to explain why they are not overcome by the toxic sulfur fumes, except to surmise that they have built up a tolerance over the years. Although they fly in pairs, sometimes they join large flocks.*

*On my first Sunday in Nicaragua a flock of green parrots flew into the large tree behind the church. They were so noisy that my sermon couldn't be heard over their chatter, and I had to pause until they flew away. "Does this happen every Sunday?" I asked despairingly. I was told that it had never happened before, and it never happened again until my last Sunday service five years later.*

*The parrots returned as if they had come to welcome me and came back to say farewell. Some things in Nature, like some things in the spiritual realm of human affairs, cannot be easily explained, although we may imagine our own allegories.*

∽

*On the opposite side of the Pan American Highway from the Union-St. Francis Church in Managua and across a fallow field, the head of the U.S. Air Force Advisory Mission in Nicaragua rented a house for his family. At any time of the year, but especially at the height of the dry season, when clouds of dust filled the air and darkened the sky, a stroll to the Adams' home after a day in the church office and a glass of limeade on their verandah offered respite and refreshment.*

*Martha Adams went inside to answer the ringing telephone and left me alone in the shade of the porch beside the swimming pool. The cougar slipped between the trees and crouched on the other side of the pool to lap up water. Her muscles and sinews rippled underneath her beautiful tawny coat; and as she looked up at me, she was so close that I could almost see the pupils of her yellow eyes. I looked back at her aware that she could observe me as closely and clearly as I saw her; but her dehydration was greater than her fear in the drought, especially severe that year; and my fascination was greater than my fear. When she slacked her thirst, she slipped away back between the trees as silently and powerfully as she had come.*

*More than three decades later Rilla and I were cruising in Alaska on my retirement trip. We'd chosen a small ship that could sail close to the shoreline and would be willing to stop to see wild life. A cow moose and her calf swam across a broad inlet. The calf would lag behind the mother, and she would swim around and nudge her calf forward. Several times the calf slipped below the surface of the water, and there would be a collective gasp from everyone on board the ship, and then the cow's nuzzle would push the calf up. For over a half an hour the ship waited and watched them. At last the cow climbed over the rocks and up the bank onto the shore; but there was no sign of the calf. The naturalist on board told us that the cow was almost certainly escaping from a predator, a wolf or a bear that she could have handled for her own safety but from which she would have been unable to protect her calf. Then the calf pulled up unsteadily on the rocks with great effort and stumbled onto the ledge on wobbly legs, only a few weeks old. The cheers and applause from the ship would have rivaled the most raucous football crowd in Alabama after a winning touchdown.*

*The risk and courage of animals in the wild remind us together with the risk and courage of the heroes of our own kind about some of the best qualities of what it means to be human.*

∽

*For several years before the major earthquake that destroyed Managua in 1972 there had been smaller quakes that did considerable damage to the city and the surrounding Nicaraguan countryside. One morning after an especially severe quake the previous night I went into the kitchen and found Emmalina, our housekeeper, in tears. When I inquired about her house and family and friends and learning that they were all unaffected, I asked her why she was weeping. "I just feel so sorry for the rich people," she told me.*

*"Well, what about the poor people, Emmalina?"*

*"Oh, Don Juan (what she called me), they can build their houses again in a few days; but the rich people may not get back into their homes for months and months."*

∽

*One year while I lived in Nicaragua the rainy season did not arrive at the usual time following an especially severe drought. People in the villages on the east coast were starving, and Church World Service sent tons of rice and beans, but it was my task to get them transported from Managua across the continent. I appealed to our U. S. military officers, but no American aircraft was readily available. They arranged with the Nicaraguan Air Force for a plane. I don't know the makes and numbers of aircraft, but it was a two propellor plane with an open door across which a chain was strung that rattled and jangled throughout the flight.*

*The rainy season seemed to begin even as we flew; and as it often starts, with a vengeance. The airplane tossed and dipped suddenly in the storm. Colonel Bill Francisco, the head of the U. S. military advisory mission in Nicaragua, accompanied us; and he went up to the cockpit to evaluate the situation. When he returned, he said "John, you go on up to the cockpit and look down at that little mud puddle where we're supposed to land, and then you come back, and let's us do some responsive readings."*

*We prayed. The storm abated. We landed. The village elders received the bags of rice and beans and avoided starvation. Even before my Celtic studies supplied descriptions and theologies I had experienced the mystery and power, the cruelty and benevolence of Nature.*

❧

*Before I married, Floyd Avary and I with two salaries were able to employ both a housekeeper and a gardener for the house we shared in Managua. A young man in his late teens named Carlos had appeared at our gate and asked to work for us when he heard that we were looking for a gardener. Floyd and I tutored him in reading and math to elevate his rudimentary skills, and it soon became apparent that Carlos was too bright and too industrious to spend his life as a gardener. Floyd arranged for him to be apprenticed in a factory with the possibility of quickly rising to a foreman's position.*

*After several weeks Carlos appeared at our front door again. "Don Floyd, Don Juan (what he called me), please don't make me stay in that dark, smelly place any longer, where I never see the sun. If you'll just let me come back and work for you, you won't have to pay me as much as you did before." We took him back and raised his salary but regretted that he might never have the opportunity again to fulfill his potential.*

*When Floyd was called back to the home headquarters of his company in the United States I could no longer afford to pay two people to care for my home. Emmalina, my housekeeper, was aging and experiencing health problems and wanted to retire. In those days one person had to be at the house to prevent thieves from breaking in and carrying everything away. Carlos declared that he could cook for me and clean the house as well as tend the garden. Some of the food that he prepared at first was strange and almost unpalatable, but Carlos was a quick study in cooking as in everything else.*

*While I was in the United States for my wedding, my house was broken into; and members of my congregation felt certain that Carlos, who had been asleep in his room beside the kitchen, was in on the job. A member of the U.S. military support mission had arranged for a soldier from the Nicaraguan National Guard to sit on my front porch with a tommy gun across his lap, which presented an impression utterly opposed to the image that I wished to convey as a Christian pastor. All the way home from the airport after our honeymoon the friends who picked us up tried to convince Rilla that Carlos would murder her in her sleep if she stayed in our house in the remote campo. I was determined that my bride and I would stay together in our home that night. Poor Rilla was caught in between, but she stayed in our home for her first night in Nicaragua as a married woman. The next morning I gave the Nicaraguan soldier his walking papers. I knew how soundly Carlos slept, and the robbers had broken into the opposite end of the house from his bedroom.*

*When Rilla and I moved to the Episcopal church's rectory, where a staff was already in place, we no longer needed Carlos. I arranged for him to be the custodian at the Episcopal diocesan office in Managua. Before he agreed to accept what I thought would be, for the second time, a wonderful opportunity for him, Carlos wanted to know if he would be able to see the sun or would have to stay inside all day. I assured him that the grounds and gardens around the office building would require much care and he would have the opportunity to see the sun for many hours each day.*

❧

*For several months before Carlos began working for us in Managua, our garden was tended by Don Julio, who was the father of our housekeeper. Emmalina seemed old to me—perhaps everyone over forty seems old to us in our twenties–and her father, Don Julio, seemed ancient. Poverty, illness, and hard labor in the developing world give the appearance of old age to people who may look decades older than their chronological age.*

*Don Julio could not write his name, but out of respect for his age everyone used the honorific "Don" in addressing him. Emmalina wrote out our grocery lists using very creative phonetic spelling. Her sons studied at the university. Her father's full name was Julio Cesar Zapato—roughly translated Julius Caesar Shoe—but in spite of his name he had never worn shoes. Every morning he hiked down into the volcanic lagoon behind our house to bathe. It seemed a pointless exercise to me. Surely he perspired more sweat in climbing back up the steep bank of the lagoon than he had washed away. I suggested that he use Emmalina's shower beside her room; but he maintained that bathing indoors was bad for your health, that he had bathed in the lagoon every day of his life and would continue to do so until he died.*

*Through Emmalina I became acquainted with many other folk traditions. She refused to iron clothes and open a refrigerator door on the same day, because she believed it would cause arthritis. (I suspected it also had the advantage of keeping her from preparing food and doing laundry on the same day.)*

*We had an avocado tree in the back yard that had never borne fruit. I told Don Julio to cut it down so that we could plant something else in its place. He told me that it was the wrong sex, and we should make it into a female. When I inquired how we would do that, he said we had to "circuncidar" the tree. I went into the house to look the unfamiliar word* up in the dictionary and learned that it meant "to circumcise." I went back outside and asked him how you circumcised a tree, adding that the purpose of circumcising human males was not intended to change their gender. He said he would cut out a ring of bark about a finger's width all around the trunk of the tree. I thought that it would certainly die soon from that procedure and we could then replace it. I should have realized that anything with a grain of life in it grows in Nicaragua from seeing the fence posts around pastures that have sprouted limbs and leaves. The next rainy season the avocado tree bore fruit, and we never lacked for avocados.

Don Julio also claimed that if human females climbed into fruit trees after they began to have sexual relations, the trees would become sterile. So long as they remained virgins even following puberty, the trees would continue to bear fruit after the women climbed in them. When I related the miracle of the avocado tree and Don Julio's folk wisdom about virgins and fruit trees, my friends with teenaged daughters made a close examination of their orchards after the girls had climbed up to gather the fruit.

We learn about Nature not only from scientists with doctoral degrees but sometimes also from shoeless peasants, even one named "Shoe."

∽

For a long time I'd wanted to visit a missionary priest friend on the Pearl Lagoon, one of the most remote areas of Nicaragua, on the Miskito Coast (so named for the Indian tribe, not for the insects). David McCallum was a gracious host who made the best stroganoff I'd ever tasted using turtle meat and combining Indian and European recipes. (The Indian villages around the Pearl Lagoon focused much of their culture on turtles.)

One afternoon David suggested that I take the small non-motorized dugout canoe and paddle through the swamps at the edge of the lagoon. The birds and vegetation were remarkable enough, but soon I found myself in a breathlessly spectacular area like a very large room filled with thousands of orchids in bloom hanging from the trees. I began to gather *them and place them around me in the cavity of the canoe until it was almost filled. Long years before ecological and environmental theology sensitized me I began to feel a twinge of regret and shame. We should not waste the beauty of Nature merely to flatter and delight ourselves, even in its extravagant plenitude.*

❧

The Union Church sponsored a Boy Scout troop; and I tried to visit the weekend camp-outs, although I rarely spent the night, because a good rest and sound sleep on Saturday nights were sacrosanct before Sunday services. One of the scouts' favorite camp sites was at Jíloa on the opposite side of the lagoon from the road to Managua, where the underwater vents of sulfur bubbled through the dark water and a colony of wild monkeys provided the evening entertainment.

One Saturday night I stayed longer than I usually allowed myself to do—my sermon must have been prepared and polished early that week. I ate supper with the boys, who often roasted iguanas over the campfire. Floyd was their Scoutmaster; but one of the adult chaperones offered to take me back across the lake in a small boat, so that Floyd's big boat could remain docked. We were in the middle of the lagoon when a thunderstorm unexpectedly blew up with the sudden fury typical of the tropics. The little boat heaved and tossed and rolled. It was one of the dozen or so times I thought I would surely die, and it gave me a new empathy for Jesus' disciples caught in the storm on the Sea of Galilee and a new appreciation of how Jesus calmed the thundering winds and roiling waters.

❧

*My soul friends over the years have often differed from me in temperament, perspective, social and political allegiance, and various other ways; but we have always enjoyed some common interest or project. John Davis and I shared the joys and frustrations of working with teenagers. Harris Cornett and I were involved together in interfaith dialogue. Floyd Avary, with whom I shared a house in Nicaragua before I was married and who shaped my life more than any other friend, introduced me to bird watching.*

*Floyd and I rented a house from a French family that had built a finca in the campo far away from main roads. From our back patio we daily watched anis, grackles, royal jays, scissortails, motmots and flocks of parrots among other tropical birds and seasonally enjoyed the migratory birds that move back and forth to and from North and South America through the narrow passage of Central America. Scattered crumbs just outside the French doors of the dining room brought indigo and painted buntings almost to our feet. When Rilla and I married, the wedding gift from Floyd's parents, who had spent most of their married life in Central America, was a pair of binoculars, so that we might share the company of birds as they had done.*

*In more recent years my close contact with wild feathered creatures has been with the tiniest of their kind, hummingbirds. In our retirement home two feeders in our courtyard attract them only a few yards from where I sit each morning reading the newspaper. Despite being the smallest of the warm bloodied creatures of Nature, they are also among the most aggressive. A male often perches on the wrought iron feeder stand above the bottles of nectar to chase off all other males and any females except his mate as he puffs in and out his brilliant red chest. Despite his bravado with other birds, he is wary of me and comes near only when he whooshes over my head, almost rippling my hair, in a chase. The females are more tolerant of one another, at least some of the time. As many as three have fed together at one of the bottles of nectar with as many as seven flitting about in the patio. The females are also more curious about me and our poodle Chérie at my feet and may fly within a few feet of my face and hover like tiny helicopters to examine us. When I'm refilling the feeder they may circle above my head in impatience.*

*I delight in their beauty, like living, moving pieces of iridescent jewelry; and I marvel at their aerobatic displays, but I find their greed and envy and competition too reminiscent of some of the worst of human qualities. Their fear of not getting enough, even though I never let the feeders go dry, and their promotion of their family against others are unattractive features of such lovely creatures. Even with the provision of abundance and plenty they act as if they are facing great scarcity and threatened survival, like many in the human tribe.*

❧

*Poverty was all around me as a child, but I never recognized it. The four tenant families on our farm lived in much smaller houses than ours; but we all slept in cold, unheated bedrooms in the winter under piles of quilts. No one went hungry; and I much preferred to eat what Tom cooked in pots over his fireplace or in the McFarlands' kitchen than in our house—somehow their food always tasted better.*

*My greatest delight was having supper and spending the night at the McFarlands' home with Bob and George, who were just older and just younger than I was. After I described Mrs. McFarland's feast—she was called "Fronie" by my family rather than addressed with her formal name, "Sofronia"—my mother told me that I could no longer have supper there. I could still spend the night on Friday or Saturday, but I had to go down after supper. She said that if I told Mrs. McFarland that she had forbidden me from eating with them I would never be allowed to spend the night there again. I was to say, "I have something to do with my family, so I'll have to come down after supper." I agreed to her terms and scrupulously followed them lest I be denied the great joy of George and Bob's companionship. I thought that there must be something in Mrs. McFarland's food that was bad for me.*

OUR DELEGATION TO THE VILLAGE *on the Pearl Lagoon on Nicaragua's Miskito East Coast arrived during the brief twilight between the blazing day and the ebony night. Darkness falls suddenly and dramatically in the tropics. As we made our way from the motorized dugout canoe we could smell the feast prepared for us as the smoke of camp fires wafted between the torches interspersed among the palm trees. We ate the delicious roasted chicken and plantains off banana leaves. The taste was delectable, but I had difficulty swallowing each bite.*

*The villagers did not share in the repast that they had prepared for us. We were consuming their supply of protein for the week, perhaps for the month. Their impulse to give, to share, to show hospitality and honor and affection was greater than their anxiety about where they would find their next meal. We had to eat to show our gratitude, our appreciation, our communion. Was I chewing up the hen that would have laid an egg for the toddler who smiled at me with big black eyes and clapping brown hands? My body was well fed, but I had difficulty digesting it spiritually. It is inspiring to observe people who give every-thing in love and horde nothing for themselves. It is troubling to be the recipient of that gift.*

*WHEN I CAME BACK to the U. S. A. for home leave a few months later, I asked my mother if there had been something in Mrs. McFarland's food that was bad for me all those years ago, although now I believed I already knew the answer and Mother's reason for denying me supper at Bob and George's home. "No, son, not at all. When you told me about all Mrs. McFarland served you . . . (pickled peaches and string beans and fried chicken and ham and press meat and blackberry jam with butter to put on her big fluffy biscuits), I knew that she was opening up things they'd canned and cured for the winter and might not have enough to last them if they put it all out for you every time."*

∽

*The last four months of 2005 and much of 2006 were among the most anxious times of our lives. Lauren and Neill lost their home and jobs and most of their possessions in New Orleans from the devastation of Hurricane Katrina. They lived like gypsies with us and Neill's parents and made forays back to Louisiana to rescue their pets—their dog and one of their cats survived—and reclaim some personal items that weren't ruined and deal with insurance and repairs for their house. They shared the even greater woe of some of their friends—the mother-in-law of one of Lauren's bridesmaids spent forty-eight hours on an interstate overpass without food or water or toilet facilities after being evacuated from the roof of her home.*

*Eventually Lauren and Neill and Lennox relocated to Durham, North Carolina; and a year later Rilla and I bought a house in a nearby county. Rilla was an only child, and Lauren is an only child. Rilla's father once said that he'd noticed on the farm that if a hen had lots of chicks she would lift her wings and cluck and the chicks would scamper toward her but that if the old biddy had only one chick she would run herself ragged all over the barnyard chasing that single chick. The Carters spent every major holiday with us, even in Nicaragua and France. We now live a half hour's drive away from Lauren and Neill and our grandchildren.*

*In the face of the violence and destruction of Nature, it's comforting to recall some of Nature's gentler parables.*

# Recognizing Humanity
# Within Ourselves

*" . . . what human being knows what is truly human except the human spirit that is within?"* — I Corinthians 2: 11 (NRSV)

*" . . . now we see in a mirror dimly, but then we will see face to face. Now I know only in part; then I will know, even as I have been fully known."* — I Corinthians 13: 12 (NRSV)

*"The Spirit bears witness with our spirit that we are children of God."* — Romans 8: 16 (NRSV, alternate reading)

The first three sections of this book could have been discussed in any sequence and order. I chose to begin with other people, because personal encounters have had the greatest influence on my own exploration of what it means to be human. This section must follow the other three, however, because pondering the inner life relies on the interpretations of our experiences in the outward world. What is sometimes pejoratively called "navel gazing" involves more than examining our own navels, either literally or metaphorically. The final step in understanding what it means to be human is taken by meditating on our own humanity as shaped and clarified by our relationships with other people, by human history, and by Nature.

When we withdraw to consider the truth or falsity of how other people have defined and categorized us, we assess the humanity of our inner self. When we study the virtues and failures of historical and literary figures, we measure our own virtues and failures by their stature. When we draw apart to a lonely place in the natural world, we ponder our place and thereby humanity's role in the whole created order. And in all these situations and circumstances, when we are alone and apart, Jesus is our model and guide for the full, perfect, complete humanity of the inner self, as he was our guide in discerning true humanity in personal relationships, in history, and in Nature.

A perennial element in our conversation with our inner self is the debate between how other people perceive us and how we understand ourselves. At times others may judge us more realistically and objectively than we see ourselves. More often, however, the ways we are stereotyped conflict with an inner sense of our true self. Jesus was often misunderstood as a blasphemer by those who opposed him,[1] but he seemed to be more troubled by those who followed him yet misinterpreted his Messianic vocation.[2] Jesus referred to himself most often as the "son of man," which is an especially important designation for our inquiry, because in the traditional usage of his time it referred not just to humanity but also to a vision of perfected humanity.[3]

In my own life I have been annoyed by people who have criticized me unjustly or disparaged me in ways that I believe are wrong. I have been accused of being controlling and domineering, when I have pressed for solutions and resolutions to issues. Some of the accusations must be accepted as justified, if exaggerated and distorted; but much of the inner dialogue of the self is involved in sifting what is true and what is false in people's complaints about us. Much greater difficulties for inner discernment result from the wishful projections onto us from those who love and admire us. Perhaps the clergy are especially vulnerable to fantasies of projected goodness and virtue. Too often those projections do not even involve the moral qualities to which we might aspire but rather make assumptions about presumed habits of petty moralism and provincial conformity. ("Don't say that . . . do that in front of

---

1   Matthew 9: 3; 26:65; Mark 14:64; John 10: 33

2   Emphasized in Mark's Gospel, but found in all four Gospels.

3   In the book of Enoch the title "Son of Man" was interchangeable with "Elect One" or "Anointed One" which was equivalent to "Christ" or "Messiah." Edwin Lewis, "Son of Man," p. 697, *Harper's Bible Dictionary*, sixth edition, 1959, Harper and Brothers, New York

the preacher!") Still more perplexing are attributions to undeserved wisdom, piety, and virtue. Those who have held me in an esteem and honor greater than I believe I deserve often drove me to an inventory of my inner self—who I truly am and who I aspire to become, what is the integrity of my humanity and what nascent qualities in my life are most crucial for the attainment of true and full humanity.

The qualities of the inner life that Jesus valued are collected from his teachings by Matthew in what is familiarly called "The Sermon on the Mount,"[4] especially in its introduction in the Beatitudes.[5] Volumes have been written about what the Beatitudes mean and imply; but however they are interpreted, a majority of them refer to virtues of the inner life—poverty of spirit, mourning, meekness, hungering and thirsting for righteousness, purity of heart—rather than to activities of outward behavior.

Many people have speculated about the meaning of purity of heart, but all of them contrast its inner spiritual quality with outward actions. Mourning may seem a strange description for a virtue of the inner life; but when the heart is broken, mourning often creates an inward opening for spiritual insight. (Later I shall list other crises and turning points of life that evoke explorations of the inner life.) The difference is evident between hungering and thirsting for righteousness and giving the appearance of righteousness. The deep longing to attain a righteousness, not yet perfected, is emphasized rather than merely following prescribed commandments and statutes in outward conduct. At no time does Jesus denigrate virtuous conduct, but he shows the importance of consistency between behavior and intention. It is not enough to refrain from adultery but also to monitor feelings of lust.[6] Enemies are to be treated not only with justice but also to be loved.[7] This purity of spiritual intention is described as imitating God who

---

4  Matthew chapters 5-7
5  Matthew 5: 1-12
6  Matthew 5: 27-28
7  Matthew 5: 28-47

is perfect.[8] Jesus warns about practicing piety before others just to be seen by them and provides examples in the practices of almsgiving and prayer.[9] Forgiveness, a matter of the heart, is primary and paramount for discipleship.[10] Freedom from anxiety involves trust as well as setting proper priorities.[11] Restraint from judging others results from inward examination of the self.[12]

The Sermon on the Mount concludes, however, with the admonition that not only must intentions be consistent with actions but also just as crucially that actions be consistent with intentions. "Not everyone who says 'Lord, Lord' will enter the kingdom of heaven, but only the one who does the will of my Father in heaven."[13] The final parable in the Sermon on the Mount emphasizes that everyone who hears Jesus' words must *act* on them.[14]

The conflict between Jesus and the Pharisees centered on the contrast between outward behavior and inner motivation. Jesus did note the occasional inconsistencies between what the Pharisees taught and how they behaved, but both historical analysis and Jesus' observations confirm that the Pharisees usually practiced what they preached. The greater concern for Jesus was the contrast between outwardly righteous actions and the paucity of inward sentiments of mercy, faith, and love. His accusation of hypocrisy against the Pharisees has more to do with

---

8  Matthew 5: 48 The word "perfect" is *teleios*, which means bringing to completion and final accomplishment and thus implies for human beings a movement toward the end and goal of life. As noted in footnote 36 in the chapter on History, this is the same word that is used in the Definition of the Council of Chalcedon for "perfect" man and "perfect" God in Christ. In English the word "teleology" means "being directed toward an end or shaped by a purpose." p. 1025 *Webster's Collegiate Dictionary*, fifth edition, 1947, G. & C. Merriam Co. Springfield, Massachusetts. Also noted above, the word that Luke uses to translate Jesus' mandate is merciful (*oiktirmos*), so we may assume that in Christianity perfection and mercy have much in common.

9  Matthew 6: 1-6

10 Matthew 6: 14-15

11 Matthew 6: 25-33

12 Matthew 7: 1-5

13 Matthew 7: 21

14 Matthew 7: 24

the inconsistency between their inner life and their outward behavior than between their words and their actions, and so he called them "whitewashed tombs."[15]

In the sense of inconsistency between inner feelings and outward actions, most of us can justly be called hypocrites more often than the times we have said one thing and done another. It is this conflict between our public behavior and our inmost, secret thoughts that drives us to examine our consciences and ask ourselves who we really are and how our humanity has failed to develop. Perhaps no group of people are more tempted to hypocrisy in that sense than the clergy, not because they act in ways contrary to what they teach, but because they conform to patterns of conventional deportment in order to "keep the peace" that may differ from what they feel and think inwardly. Contemporary ordained Christians like their pious predecessors of the first century may be the ultimate modern pharisees. In addition to the impulses toward developing and perfecting our humanity that arise from the visions and aspirations of our vocation, the clergy are forced to ponder the true virtues and righteous aspirations of our hearts that arise in tension with our public roles.

Heightened moments that explode suddenly and without warning in the stream of daily life—conflict, danger, threat, disappointment, failure, as well as joy, success, inspiration, interpersonal communion, expressed affection—often drive us to withdraw from the busy world and look inward. What did I do to cause the rupture in a relationship, and what in me elicits such hostility? What is my life worth as it is almost taken away? Am I more than the sum of my achievements or less than my humiliations? Do I deserve the happiness that fills me or the sadness that overwhelms me? Each of these occasions impels me to ask who I truly am and what are the nature and distortion of my humanity. In a similar way, life-turning events—marriage, vocational change, births of children and grandchildren, deaths of family members and friends—result in making us question our identity and weigh the progress of our developing humanity.

---

15 Matthew 23: 27; see the full context in Matthew 23: 1-36

Jesus was driven to look within himself as he anticipated the beginning of his public ministry and retreated for forty days alone in the wilderness where he was tempted to an inauthentic messiahship and to deny the reality of his humanity. As he anticipated his death he once again questioned his place in human history and wanted to evade the pain and responsibility of completing his purpose as the first fully perfect human being. Satan tempted Jesus to achieve desirable results through supernatural means, thus denying the instrumentality of his humanity (and thereby negatng the Incarnation).[16]

In the garden of Gethsemene Jesus prayed to be exempted from the consequent burden that resulted from his having carried out the vocation of living a complete and perfect human life. In asking "if it be possible" to remove the cup of suffering and death, Jesus asked if it would be possible to live a perfect and full human life without facing suffering and death; and of course, the answer he found from God within himself was "no, it is not possible."[17]

My decision to go to seminary rather law school, my marriage, the births of our daughter and our grandchildren, the death of my parents and others, especially a young friend who had been my protégé,[18] my first experiences of failure and success in coition and failure and success in procreation, my wife's chronic illnesses, near successes and ultimate failures to publish my novels, the decision to move from Baptist to Episcopal ministry, various times I considered leaving the ordained ministry, retirement, all produced days of heightened sensitivity that provoked an inward reflection about my human role and identity and worth and purpose.

In more tranquil and less eventful periods of my life, I was often spurred to inward reflections by passages from novels and short stories and scenes from plays and movies. Fictional literature has always played a large role in my thoughts and feelings, both as a writer and

---

16  Matthew 4: 1-11; Luke 4: 1-13

17  Luke 22: 42-44

18  See the reference to "mourning" in the Beatitudes above and the vignette about Hank in the chapter about "Others."

as a reader and observer. In ways similar to the roles of art, music, and poetry as surrogates for Nature, the roles of novels, stories, dramas, and movies acted as surrogates for lived experiences and drove me to momentary reflections on my identity and humanity. To be sure, fictional literature and stage and screen productions can open our eyes to a wider world outside ourselves; and art, music, and poetry can plunge us into inward meditation; but for me an identification with fictional characters and situations usually resulted in inner reflection while visual art, music, and poetry propelled me to thoughts and feelings about the world outside myself.

While the failure to publish any of my novels had a profound influence on my sense of personal worth, the process of writing them also contributed to my self-understanding. My first novel was written during my senior year of college, when I was given two semesters of credit as an experiment in self study.[19] It was an idealized romance and reflected my own struggles with gender relationships and sexuality. The second novel was written during my years at seminary and also had a romantic, although somewhat gothic theme, that centered on the relationship of an unattractive, obese woman and a strikingly handsome retarded man. Feelings about my own inadequacies were surely projected into both of those characters. During my last year of seminary and during my first years of ministry I wrote a novel about racial relations in the Southern United States at the same time I was also involved in the Civil Rights Movement. It was a more mature work that received attention from New York publishers and also the University of Alabama Press, although ultimately it was never published. My fourth novel was written in Nicaragua and France and dealt with the conflict of cultures in post colonial Central America and was set during the Epiphany season with accompanying religious references and symbols. Like the third novel my devoted agents got it read by many New York publishers but without any final success. The last novel was more an exercise that perhaps prepared for this memoir. Although it was read

---

19 There is some irony in my being granted credit for "self study," which turned out to be the only benefit for the experiment.

by the friend who is publishing this book, I made no serious efforts to have it published. It attempted to retell some of the incidents from Jesus' ministry in contemporary America with a female protagonist. A subplot of my final novel also explored the struggle of gays and lesbians to receive dignity and justice. Perhaps because I support that cause but have become too old to attack the barricades, as I did in my youth in seeking racial equality, I have become merely an armchair advocate. I see many parallels between the Civil Rights Movement that was waged when my ministry and writing were beginning and the contemporary concerns about discrimination due to sexuality and gender. Although none of my novels was intentionally autobiographical, all of them sought to understand what it means to be human and forced me to consider my own humanity in relation to the characters that I had created whose inner lives, often very different from my own, I sought to understand.

The triggers for inner reflection may sometimes result from overlapping impulses arising from different contexts. A crisis or tragedy or failure has often impelled me to venture alone into a numinous place in the natural world, where I would find not only spiritual balm but also insight. There seems to be something about going apart into the natural world at times when we are "wearied by the changes and chances of this life"[20] that inspire inward reflection. It was in the wilderness that Elijah heard the "still small voice," which may be better expressed as the sound of absolute silence, and so gained a new perspective;[21] and as noted several times earlier Jesus often withdrew to a lonely place in the natural world, especially after periods of stress and exhaustion.

Although flashes of self-understanding may be gained at times when we are driven by heightened emotions or surprised by sudden events or awed by spectacular beauty, however, a greater insight into our inner humanity may be derived from intentional practices of spiritual discipline. The individual insights of daily devotions may be less dramatic than the sudden revelations we receive at memorable

---

20 From a collect in the service of Compline, p. 133, The Book of Common Prayer
21 I Kings 19: 12

moments in our lives, but the cumulative growth in awareness may ultimately result in a deeper and fuller knowledge of the humanity of the inner self. Several practices have been important for me at various times in my life. Some have lasted for several months, some for several years, others have shaped lifelong habits of the heart.

Twice I engaged in sessions of psychotherapy, once for a few months, the other time for a couple of years. Both were initiated by attempts to find relief from depression and anxiety, and both followed periods of extreme vocational and familial stress. The longer therapy occurred during the terminal illnesses and deaths of my father and father-in-law, when I was also considering leaving pastoral ministry for another vocation inside or outside the church and when I faced the final rejection of a novel that I had worked on for a number of years that had earlier received encouragement from publishers. The weekly talk therapy and psycho tropic medications allowed me to continue to function and carry on with daily activities as well as to make important decisions for future change. Psychotherapy also helped me to share openly and honestly both in formalized sacramental confession and in less formal intimate conversation with colleagues and close friends. The unburdening of my mind and heart in conversations with friends and family members has been important throughout my life and has probably had a larger impact with greater continuity than my experiences either in psychotherapy or sacramental confession, although all three modes have enhanced and benefited the others

The most momentous spiritual experience of my life from at least my second decade into my eighth decade has been prayer, although prayer has taken many diverse forms and evolved into various shapes over the years. My practice of prayer began, as likely many other people's did, as pleas and requests to God for myself and for friends and family members and the world. Certainly those daily petitions and intercessions have never ceased, but over the years other kinds of prayer have contributed much more to an understanding of my humanity and so to what it means to be human.

During the same period of stress and emotional disturbance when

I was driven to seek help from psychotherapy, Rilla and I attended a
clergy conference led by Mark Dyer.[22] I do not remember the subject
of the conference; but after the planned program was concluded, Mark
Dyer and several couples stayed an extra night at our diocesan camp [23]
for scheduling reasons, and somehow an informal conversation led to
his description and demonstration of how to use the "Jesus prayer."[24]
All my life I have been plagued by insomnia, and during this period
my sleeplessness was especially acute and was one of the main factors
that caused me to seek psychiatric help, because I was sleeping very
little at night. Although it took a few days of practice for me to learn to
use the Jesus prayer and several weeks for it to become a reflexive part
of my breathing, it changed my life. I slept more as my mind repeated,
"Lord Jesus, Son of God," (as I inhaled) and "have mercy on me a sin-
ner," (as I exhaled); but even when I slept only a few hours, I felt more
relaxed and rested and even refreshed during the next day.

Eventually the Jesus prayer was insinuated into the waking hours
of daytime as well—when stuck in traffic, when waiting in line or
"holding" on the telephone. Somehow the subconscious strengths of
my inner faith supplied trust and courage to my outward responses
and activities. "Quietness and confidence"[25] gave me strength to face
and overcome "the cares and occupations of life."[26]

The Jesus prayer has continued to balance and nourish my daily
life. Almost every night I fall asleep as it emerges from my subcon-
sciousness, without effort or intentional practice; and often during idle
times that might otherwise cause fretting frustration, it flows into my
mind uninvited and unprompted as I breathe in and out. Although I
am grateful for the temporary relief that psychotherapy and medications offered, so that I could function and then get on fully with my

---

22 This happened before the Rev. Mark Dyer was consecrated as a bishop, when he
   was the spiritual director for the Episcopal Diocese of Massachusetts.

23 Camp McDowell, Diocese of Alabama, Nauvoo, Alabama

24 The "Jesus Prayer" is a form of meditation from the tradition of the Russian Orthodox Church.

25 The Book of Common Prayer, p. 832

26 The Book of Common Prayer, p. 57

activities, the use of the Jesus prayer has provided a greater long-term impact on my life.

The Jesus prayer was my first experience, other than academically or conceptually, with any form of meditation or contemplation; but it led me to explore others, both visual images, such as picturing the 23rd psalm and other shepherd themes without words, as I felt myself being held and carried by a divine shepherd, contemplating icons, and also simply resting in silence and quietness touched by, surrounded by, upheld by a divine presence.[27]

What all kinds of meditative and contemplative prayer taught me about being human was the recognition of a God-shaped hole within myself that can only be filled and satisfied with a divine presence. The understanding and acknowledgment of this God-shaped hole in the psyche suggest one of the most important and distinctive elements of what it means to be human.

Classical Christian faith has professed that this God-shaped hole in Jesus was constantly and perfectly and completely filled with God Himself, while in the rest of us it is only partially and distortedly and sporadically occupied by a divine presence. Thus Jesus is described in the creeds as truly God and truly man, as noted in the introduction above. Although an exploration of Jesus' full divinity is beyond the scope of this book and ultimately beyond the kin of our understanding, the God-shaped hole in us, which perhaps more than anything else defines what it is to be human, especially links us to the perfect man Jesus, in whom the full and complete divine presence always dwelt.

A better understanding achieved through mediative and contemplative prayer of the God-shaped hole within me, which had been intimated but not understood earlier in my life, led to changes in other practices of prayer. The petitions and intercessions in which I told God what I wanted and needed for myself and other people and

27 This kind of prayer resembles "Centering Prayer," in which I have participated in groups on several occasions; but I have had no formal training in the discipline and hesitate to say that I observe it correctly. See a similar caveat below with regard to *lectio divina*.

the world were transformed, although imperfectly with frequent failures and regressions, into efforts to hold myself and others and world situations before the divine presence and wait quietly and silently for inspiration and insight.

My habitual routine of petition and intercession that supplements the Daily Office begins with a Buddhist prayer that I came across during my involvement with the antinuclear peace movement:

> Lord, lead me from death to life,
> from falsehood to truth,
> from despair to hope,
> from fear to trust,
> from hate to love,
> from war to peace.

I find that one of the phrases of this prayer alerts me to my present spiritual temperature, where my inner being is at that moment, much as a thermometer measures physical temperature. I then try to hold my present concerns before the divine presence, beginning with my family, followed by my friends, enemies, and those with particular needs for healing—before I retired from full time parish ministry I read serially through the parish role each week, holding all members one by one before the divine presence—then lifting up the church, beginning with leaders and colleagues and areas of local and international missionary concern; then holding up national and world trouble spots—for many years I focused on the leaders of nations by name; but I found I was distracted by my prescriptions for their roles, so I now think more geographically than personally, asking that God's will be done. Finally I ask God's guidance for my future activity by rehearsing the liturgical year:

Bring prophetic promise to my life (Advent);
Plant new seeds of grace in my heart (Christmas);
Inspire, enlighten, equip, prepare my heart (Epiphany);
Forgive, redeem, restore, cleanse, absolve, pardon me (Lent);

Sanctify my suffering (Passiontide);

Grant me a rebirth in faith and a new spiritual beginning (Easter)

Then bring to fulfillment and fruition what I shall be and think and feel (Pentecost), and fill me with hope and faith and a measure of Your grace, so that I may love You more and more and find closer union with You and greater unity with others through Your love, and then may do and write and say those things that will bring Your kingdom nearer, and finally may obtain eternal life.

As with taking my spiritual temperature using the Buddhist prayer at the beginning of my petitions and intercessions, I find that my anticipation of future behavior often falls in one of the liturgical emphases—Advent, Christmas, Epiphany, Lent, Passiontide, Easter, or Pentecost—sometimes serendipitously (but more often not) corresponding to the actual season we are celebrating.

My prayers end with a confession and the "Prayer of Humble Access" and the Lord's Prayer—reversing the usual order of Anglican public worship and the Daily Office.

"Almighty God, unto whom all hearts are open, all desires known, and from whom no secrets are hid, cleanse the thoughts of my heart by the inspiration of your Holy Spirit, that I may perfectly love you and worthily magnify your holy Name . . . ."[28]

As an Episcopal priest it is embarrassing to admit that contemplative and meditative prayer led me to an appreciation of the practice of the Daily Office, a requirement once done only out of grim duty with unsurprisingly little result and minimal beneficial effect and often neglected. A combination of saying and singing the offices at Canterbury Cathedral during my sabbatical study in 1996 in the presence of the Christian community along with my growing practice of contemplative and meditative prayer brought new appreciation and regular observance of the Daily Office. The parishes where I have served as a priest afforded little opportunity for the weekday reading of the Daily Office in the company of other Christians, and in retirement those

28 The Book of Common Prayer, p. 355

opportunities are even rarer, but after my weeks at Canterbury and with a heightened awareness of spiritual prayer I am usually able to include the community of the faithful in absentia as I read the Daily Office and also to be aware of the divine presence in and through the repeated words and readings each morning.

My pilgrimage in prayer continued from the Daily Office to a new way of reading scripture. From my childhood in the Baptist Church through my years as a youth minister and a college chaplain during seminary and for five years as an ordained Baptist minister, I read the Bible regularly. The emphasis of my study, however, was on the historical and theological meaning. To be sure, I sought to relate the events of scripture to my personal life and the situations of my parishioners and family members and friends; and I looked for parallels between Biblical passages and social, national, and world events to use in my sermons. Even so, until I began a more contemplative and meditative approach to the Daily Office, I rarely saw and felt myself within the words of the Bible. I have never been tutored in the practice of *lectio divina,* and I may not use that term in a correct technical manner; but I do now often "pray" the words of the Bible as I read them, especially in the passages from the Psalter.[29] Although I still study the scriptures seeking historical and theological understanding, *lectio divina,* as I interpret that discipline, adds another dimension to my prayers and further contributes to a sense of that God-shaped hole inside me, which for me is the apogee of what it means to be human.

The most recent addition to my spiritual practice has been pilgrimage. As a child I dreamed of travel, and from college years onward traveling was my greatest extravagance. Encountering people of different cultures and seeing places of strange beauty and visiting ancient sites certainly enriched my inner life and contributed to my understanding of the variety of manifestations of humanity. Immediately after graduating from seminary I made backpacking/youth-hostelling tour of England, Scotland, France, Germany, Italy, Switzerland, Norway, Denmark, and the Netherlands. After my ordination travel was often combined with

29 See above footnote 27.

study and conferences and courses that further enhanced my appreciation of human diversity. During my years living in Nicaragua I also
traveled to Mexico, Honduras, Guatemala, El Salvador, Costa Rica,
Colombia, and Puerto Rico and later to Venezuela, Curaçao, St. Vincent,
Martinique, and the Virgin Islands. While we were living in Nice, we
visited other French regions as well as Italy and Morocco. Between our
years abroad and parish ministry in the United States Rilla and I spent
a month in Britain and a month in Spain. Shortly after returning to the
United States we joined Rilla's parents in a tour of the Greek mainland
and islands and Turkey, often focusing on Pauline sites.

Certainly there were moments of inspiration and insight into the
meaning of humanity in all these places; but it was not until participating
in a delegation to the Soviet Union in 1988 that the idea of pilgrimage
as a spiritual practice was suggested to me. Even then the emphasis was
on historical and theological study, although participation in Russian
Orthodox worship opened new visions of how differently the God-
shaped hole in people might be shaped and filled. It was not until my
sabbatical study in Israel in 1996, however, that pilgrimage became fully
developed as a spiritual practice. As I continued my time of sabbatical
leave at Canterbury and Rome and on the mission field of Honduras, I
became spiritually attached and involved in holy places. The contrast
between my earlier travel and study with spiritual pilgrimage might
be compared to my former study of scripture and *lectio divina*. To be
sure, just as I continued to read and study the Bible historically and
theologically, I also continued to learn about the history and culture
of exotic geographical settings while I enjoyed them devotionally.

For the past decade, as I approached and then entered into retirement, Celtic Christianity has become the focus of both study and
spiritual pilgrimage. I made five trips to Europe on pilgrimage, sometimes in combination with four courses and sometimes alone in my
explorations, to Northumbria, Ireland, France, Wales, and Scotland.
Apart from the courses most of my study of the Celtic saints and the
pre-Christian Celtic culture and diverse Celtic contexts took place
before and after my travels; but it was alone and apart, as in other

withdrawals to lonely places in Nature, that I discovered new aspects of my inner self and new dimensions of what it means to be human, at the site of St. Kevin's hut at Glendelough, at St. Aidan's view of the tides and horizons of Lindisfarne, at St. Patrick's vista from the high hill of Tara, at the ruins of St. Colomba's cell and chapel in Ireland and later at the site of his cell on Iona in Scotland, at St. Wilfrid's crypts at Rippon and Hexham, at the location of St. Hilda's abbey at Whitby, at St. Ninian's cave in Scotland, at the Hedda Stone at Peterborough, at Holywell and Pennat Melangell in Wales, to name only a few memorable highlights. After study, preparation, and much anticipation, often the difficulty of reaching a place, either due to travel arrangements or the physical challenge of the terrain, contributed to the numinous sense of those places where the Celtic saints' God-shaped holes had been filled with a divine presence.

An aspect of growing up from infancy to childhood to adolescence to adult maturity to old age is a cognizance of the boundary between the limitation of one's humanity and the possibility of one's freedom. A baby falls and then exults in walking. A child is restrained from running into the street but explores swinging from monkey bars. An adolescent encounters the civil statutes when old enough to drive a car but not old enough to purchase alcoholic or nicotine products, and few in modern American society avoid the thrill and humiliation of testing those restrictions. An adult must prune youthful dreams to fit possibilities of time, talent, and responsibility to one's family. Old age brings the recognition of losing functions and capacities enjoyed earlier in life. All of these situations reflect the meaning of "law" for our humanity in the broadest sense.

For Jesus this broad sense of the law that limited his humanity was expressed in his temptation in the wilderness. The three offers made by Satan to satisfy his physical need (hunger), to defy "natural" law (gravity), and to achieve worldly power would all be given to him later in one way of another.[30]

In my own life the law was experienced most acutely in the physical

---

30 Matthew 4: 1-11; Luke 4: 1-13

limitations imposed by double vision, which prevented youthful athletic endeavors and later by the failure of vocational aspirations in music and literature, which resulted from insufficient talent and discipline as well as from lack of luck and opportunity. Although my arrests and indictments by the police and the courts were minor and infrequent, they occurred in sporadic fashion often enough to symbolize universal limitations on human freedom and to remind me of the boundaries and consequences of the civil law.

In the second section (History) I referred to the Apostle Paul as the lawgiver of the new covenant much as Moses was the lawgiver of the old covenant; and in the third section (Nature) I reflected on the limitations placed on all human beings, including at least to some extent also on Jesus, by natural law. In addition to the law, however, Paul is equally preoccupied with the theme of freedom; and his discussion of the interplay between the law and freedom is intricate and intriguing. For Paul the lines between ritual law, divine law, civil law, ontological law, and natural law are often blurred. In whatever arenas of the law we experience limits, those very boundaries raise the questions of freedom and the hope of transcending our limitations.

Old age brings the awareness of what Paul calls the final sting of the law, which is death, the ultimate boundary and limitation of humanity.[31] Throughout our lives we become conscious of the inevitability of death at heightened moments of loss or threat. When a loved one dies, when we are in great danger or peril, when national or international catastrophes happen, during wars, we have a fleeting sense that we will die someday; but as one's years increase our mortality becomes a constant awareness below the surface of our other thoughts and emotions. Faith then takes on a new role in granting freedom from the fear of death.

When we consider Christ's resurrection even more than his crucifixion we are on the cusp between his human nature and his divine nature. Because the two natures cannot be divided or separated, the humanity of Jesus is subsumed into his divinity in his resurrection; but

---

31 I Corinthians 15: 56

in this mystery we have reached the limits of rational inquiry into the nature of the humanity revealed perfectly in Jesus. Resurrection is the dissolution of the limitations and boundaries of humanity, *i.e.,* the law, and thus the manifestation of complete and unhampered freedom. To share Christ's resurrection is to be incorporated into his divine-human nature,[32] a subject beyond the scope of this book and reserved for a possible future meditation on the divine nature of Christ.

Part of the shorthand phrase "eternal life" involves Christ's victory over death. Yet, eternal life has both a future and a present reference. "The one who raised the Lord Jesus *will* raise us also with Jesus, and *will* bring us . . . into his presence";[33] but "even though outward nature is wasting away, our inner nature *is being* renewed day by day."[34] As the Book of Common Prayer puts it in the Burial Office, "in the midst of life, we are in death";[35] but the statement could be truthfully reversed as well: "in the midst of death, we are in life" by sharing the divinity of the Risen Christ. Our future eternal life through the gift of sharing the divinity of the Risen Christ is beyond the scope of this inquiry, as stated above; but our present foretaste of eternal life in our inner spiritual vitality is the gift of sharing the humanity of the incarnate and Risen Christ.

Even though Paul's expedient ministry was devoted to freeing the Gentiles from exclusion to the promises of the divine covenant, he expressed the pinnacle of human freedom in Christ as the freedom from the ultimate curse of the law in death. "The sting of death is sin, and the power of sin is the law."[36] "The last enemy to be destroyed is death."[37] "In Christ Jesus you are set free from the law of sin and death." [38] In paraphrasing Isaiah 25: 8, which looks forward to a future when death

---

32  Note the etymological connection of incorporate to "corpus" as being assimilated into a "body" or "enfleshed" as in the doctrine of the Incarnation.

33  II Corinthians 4: 14

34  II Corinthians 4: 16

35  The Book of Common Prayer, p. 484

36  I Corinthians 15: 56

37  I Corinthians 15: 26

38  Romans 8: 2

will be swallowed up, Paul gives God thanks for the victory through Jesus Christ over death in his present life.[39] Paul believes that because "Christ being raised from the dead, death will no longer have dominion over him." So we who have died to sin (and the law) with Christ will also live with him; and, therefore, even in our present earthly life, we are "alive to God in Christ Jesus" and freed from the fear of death.[40] It is from the fear of death that human freedom reaches it culmination. The release from the fear of death is surely a crowning element in the completion of our full humanity and freedom.

We begin to understand our humanity as we are able to love and be loved by other people and see our human relationships in comparison to the perfect love of Jesus. We further understand our humanity as part of a story that began centuries before our birth and will continue into the future and is clarified and illuminated by Jesus' participation at a particular time and place of history in that story. Then we understand our humanity connected to the web of all created life, of which we are but a small part, shaped by Nature but also affecting the shape of Nature, and which Jesus shared with us by becoming flesh with us. And finally we understand our humanity by looking inside ourselves, culminating in finding the God-shaped hole in us which makes us distinctively human and which was filled completely, perfectly, fully, and continually with the divine presence in Jesus.

All our images of God are metaphorical, as well as some of our images of humanity. We cannot describe God explicitly and so we cannot describe the divine presence that may enter the God-shaped hole within us.

The very phrase "God-shaped hole" is itself largely metaphorical. By using that phrase, however, I deny that human beings are immortal. We are not gods. We are tiny pieces of Nature that will dissolve and disappear. As the Ash Wednesday liturgy reminds us: "You are dust, and to dust you shall return."[41] I am also denying the Gnostic myth

---

39 I Corinthians 15: 54-55
40 Romans 6: 7-11
41 The Book of Common Prayer, p. 265

that claims a divine spark within us. We do not possess even a little fragment of divinity.

The God-shaped hole within us, however, is our most distinctively human feature. That God-shaped hole may be occupied by a divine presence, more or less, in varying ways and with diverse expressions, uniquely in every human being. For all people of various cultures and religions the divine presence within their God-shaped hole is related to whatever is of ultimate truth and meaning and has eternal value and worth. For many Christians that God-shaped hole has something to do with the resurrection of Jesus and the presence of the living Christ within them by the grace of the Holy Spirit, often mediated through the sacraments and prayer.

The presence of the living Christ within us takes us beyond a discussion of Jesus' humanity and toward a meditation on his divinity. Irenaeus is credited with saying something like "Christ became human so that we might become divine." How the distinctive human quality of possessing a God-shaped hole within us offers the possibility and hope of sharing in the life of God is involved in an inquiry about how Jesus of Nazareth who was fully, truly, and completely a man was at the same time fully, truly, completely God; and all that would be the subject for another day and a different book.

# Autobiographical Vignettes IV

*My letter of resignation as associate pastor had been self-righteously typed and defiantly folded and sealed in an envelope and proudly tucked into my inner breast coat pocket before the congregational meeting at Temple Baptist Church where a vote would be taken whether to integrate the church and allow black people (whom we called "Negroes" in those times) to become members. I congratulated myself on my willingness to sacrifice my security and salary. I exulted in my prophetic stance. I thanked God for the strength and serenity which allowed me to take such a courageous action. I marveled at how brave and noble I was in such a trying and stressful circumstance.*

*The vote was taken by secret ballot, and I reached across my heart for my letter as the result was being read. I never even considered anything but a negative response, but the congregation had voted to integrate and welcome people of all races. It revealed as much about my arrogance and lack of faith in the human goodness of other people as about the human goodness of those I had harshly prejudged.*

～

*The forecast for Sagittarius on December 31, 1969 almost made me believe in horoscopes: "Do not go out in traffic today."*

*It was forbidden to remove the altar vases from the Union-St. Francis Church, but someone had ignored the rule in order to take the Christmas flowers to a sick parishioner, and I had to retrieve them on New Year's Eve. My mood was already angry and exasperated. As I was returning to the church a car driven by the wife of a European diplomat flew back out of her driveway and slammed into my Volkswagen "bug." "No one ever comes down this road, especially on New Year's Eve," she explained. I was not amused. We called Mr. Grimm, the appropriately named Ger-*

man insurance agent employed by all of the expatriates, not so much to pay for repair bills as to keep us out of jail. (The first impulse of the Nicaraguan police after an accident with a native Nicaraguan was to jail the expatriate in hope of a bribe.) When Mr. Grimm determined that both cars could be driven, he suggested that we follow him to the body shop and get an estimate immediately.

As we arrived at kilometer five on the Pan American Highway South, close to where the insane asylum was located, we saw a totally naked adolescent boy, just beginning to sprout pubic hair, wandering in the middle of the road. The diplomat's wife and I were both able to swerve onto the shoulder, but Mr. Grimm had to stop in the middle of the road. He was attempting to get the utterly addled boy into his car when a police car—an old Mercedes like all those used exclusively by the Managua police, because Somoza, the dictator, owned the Mercedes dealership—sped over the hill and rear-ended Mr. Grimm's car. The police tried to arrest all of us, but Mr. Grimm told us to pay no attention to them and to go on to the body shop—most of us who had driven for a few years in Managua traffic were quite familiar with its location.

I lay down after returning home and taking several aspirin. Then I heard a crash. Someone who had begun New Year's Eve celebrations early with too much alcohol had crashed into the railing of the bridge in front of the church. I administered first aid and pondered what my horoscope had predicted that morning.

Some coincidences are miracles in disguise, and I believe in them, but some coincidences are just coincidences. I still don't believe in the truth of horoscopes, although I continue to read them in the daily newspaper.

◆

Great art may not always be the best symbolization for transcendent meaning. Sometimes the very beauty and charm of an object may cause us to focus on it with such rapt attention that we are not led to see through it and beyond it to a deeper reality. Doll-like plaster statues of saints may sometimes be better guides to divine truth than great sculptures. Cartoonish stained glass windows may sometimes better fracture light *into transcendent verities than exquisite gemlike transparencies.*

*I have been shocked by revelations of my humanity at moments in novels and movies and plays, which often were not celebrated literary classics. During my freshman year at Duke I saw a movie titled "The Prisoner" at the weekend campus screening staring Alec Guinness as a cardinal. It is hardly mentioned in the listing of that great actor's repertoire, but it profoundly affected my self-understanding. The movie reflects the biases of the cold war and fictionalizes the confinement of certain Roman Catholic prelates of that era in countries behind the iron curtain. The psychological and ideological devices to break the cardinal's will all fail until his tormentors strike upon the humiliation he had felt for his mother's position as a fishmonger and the associated shame experienced in the odor she could not wash from her hands, which he smelled as she held him in his early childhood, and the even greater shame he carried for having felt such humiliation about his mother. Perhaps for the first time I recognized some of my subconscious vulnerability below my rational choices, especially in feelings never articulated into thoughts about my parents.*

*Something is different about a numinous place from a scene of great natural beauty or even natural grandeur and power, although they may also be contexts for a sense of God's nearness. At the cells of Kevin at Glendalough and Columba in Ireland and in Scotland and in the footsteps of Aidan on Lindisfarne I have felt and known metaphorically the brush of angels' wings. These locations are what modern Celtic spirituality refers to as the "thin places."*

*My most potent experiences of numinous places were in the Holy Land, in the Sinai with a Bedouin tribe and in the Negev on retreat, where we were asked to find a spot out of sight of anyone but in view of a clear landmark so that we would not wander off and be lost for hours or days. The total stillness, my cool nook under a rock overhang away from the blazing, broiling sun, and the absolute silence, which might evoke a still, small voice within, related me to Moses' huddling in the cleft of a rock and Elijah fleeing to a cave and Jesus' wandering in the wilderness before his temptation. If God had spoken in audible words, it would not have been surprising. The feeling of divine presence was so tactile that I believed I could almost feel God with my fingertips if I extended my arms and hands.*

∽

*For half day excursions in Nicaragua we would go swimming at Jíloa in the volcanic lagoon or cruise through the isletas near Granada on Buck Currin's big pontoon boat, especially on Sunday afternoons. (The isletas consist of around 150 small islands that were formed when a volcano exploded in prehistoric times and spewed half of its side into the northern end of Lake Nicaragua, where the only fresh water sharks in the world and other unique sea creatures evolved after the lake was cut off from the sea and gradually became a fresh body of water.) If several days were available for an excursion we might drive up into the mountains on the Honduran border and fish for japote or persuade Willy Walker to fly us in his crop dusting plane to the San Juan river to fish for tarpon or to Omotepe for an archeological dig or take Floyd's boat to the coast and try to hook a sailfish or drive across the border to one of the beach resorts in Costa Rica.*

*A one day outing almost always involved driving over the ridge that bordered Managua to the south, where macaws might be seen flying at sunset, and down to the black volcanic sand beach on the Pacific Ocean at Pocho Mil. I spent the night at Pocho Mil only one time, when a British man, several years younger than I was, suggested camping out on the beach.*

*Late in the afternoon I decided to go for a quick swim and was immediately caught in a very strong current. As I was pulled farther and father out to sea, Ian yelled, "Are you all right, John?"*

*And I responded, "I'm fine," and waved at him. I was certain that I would die far out in the ocean, and I didn't want Ian to die, too, trying to save me; but eventually I was able to move to the edge of the current and swim diagonally back to the shore, a very long distance down the beach from our camp site. When I trudged back to our camp, Ian embraced me almost sobbing.*

*That night we lay beneath the stars and listened to the waves splashing onto the beach. Perhaps because my life had been spared, perhaps because Ian believed that I had spared his life, we told each other our deepest secrets. Never before nor since has a man looked so deeply into my soul and I into his soul. Never before nor since have I opened myself for another man to peer so deeply within me.*

~

*During my freshman year at Duke I attended a forum where a professor from North Carolina Central College University spoke. She was one of the most stylish, elegantly dressed women I had ever seen; and she told us how it felt to be well dressed, well educated, with money in her pocketbook but unable to find a place to spend the night or a decent place to eat or even a clean rest room when she drove across the South to visit her family. For me it was a revelation as shocking and stunning as the encounter with an exotic visitor from a foreign land, because it was something I'd never thought about yet often witnessed. It was the beginning of many years of my involvement in the struggle for racial justice.*

*As the pain and injustice experienced by black people due to segregation began to register on my conscience and consciousness, a few other students at Duke and I became aware of the ironic inequality of the Duke-Durham Day, sponsored by the Durham merchants association each fall before classes started. Various foods and favors and prizes, some with Duke logos, were given to students who dropped into the stores in Durham; and banners and posters were exhibited around the city welcoming Duke students back. Most Duke students brought whatever supplies they needed from their homes, while North Carolina Central students bought many school items after arriving in Durham, although there was no North Carolina Central-Durham Day for them.*

*A small group of Duke students had begun conversations with a group of North Carolina Central students about the nascent civil rights movement, just beginning to gain momentum in the late 1950s. I cannot recall how the question of the slight to North Carolina Central students first arose, but we determined to meet and discuss how the merchants might be approached to include them. A half dozen or so of us from Duke went to the North Carolina Central campus one afternoon to strategize. We began to map out a plan, but before it was finalized all the Duke students except for me had to return to our campus for a class or a lab. Jerome Dudley, the President of the North Carolina Central student body, invited me to stay and continue working out details and have supper with him in the school cafeteria. When we entered the cafeteria it seemed that every head turned toward me, the only white face in the hall; and the din of voices hushed into a silence—it seems as quiet in my memory as my Negev desert retreat forty years later, although I'm sure it was not.*

*We sent a letter to the Durham Merchants Association signed jointly by the rather fancifully self-appointed committee of both schools threatening a boycott by Duke and North Carolina Central students unless North Carolina Central was added to their welcoming day. Jerome would have been able to deliver a multitude from his campus for the boycott; I probably couldn't have mustered more than a handful of Duke students, perhaps a dozen or so.*

*Maybe the merchants knew that our threats were empty; maybe they were prompted to do the just and right thing; maybe they didn't want to jeopardize sales to North Carolina Central students; but for whatever reason they folded and acceded to our demands. Of the few successful campaigns in my life, it remains one of those in which I take the most pride.*

*Although Duke University was not yet integrated, the statewide Baptist Student Union decided to be open to students of all races. At the first convention after it was integrated I ran for state president. I asked Jerome Dudley to make my nominating address. He spoke eloquently and convincingly, and I lost the election overwhelmingly. Perhaps the convention recognized my being nominated by a black student for the hucksterism and hubris that it was.*

*As we returned to Durham we realized that we couldn't go into a restaurant together; I had not completely forgotten the speech that initiated my involvement in seeking racial justice. We were riding in Hank Irvin's car, and he and I went into a restaurant to buy take-out plates leaving Jerome and my girl friend, Katherine Batten, in the back seat together. My gullibility and naiveté had obviously still not been greatly alleviated in the two years since I heard the professor from North Carolina Central University.*

*As Hank I emerged from the restaurant we saw a group of angry young white men approaching his car. We sped away, and they followed us for a while but eventually gave up the chase. I had little of the sense of danger or peril that I experienced on other occasions when my life was in danger. We thought it had been a great adventure. Perhaps God sometimes protects naive young fools with good intentions.*

༄

*After my involvement in the Civil Rights Movement in college my friendship with my classmate Harold Thomas in seminary came as a delightful surprise. Harold was a dark skinned black man from Bermuda who was as oblivious as he was unconcerned about racial distinctions, like many of my future church members of African-Caribbean ancestry in Nicaragua.*

*During the winter of our freshman year Harold and I struggled through a snow storm to reach Georges Florovksy's patristics class, which he taught on the Harvard yard, a considerable distance from the Divinity School. Professor Florovsky with his long, flowing white beard, usually arrived wearing his black Russian Orthodox cassock and a World War II air force pilot's helmet with the earflaps pulled down and immediately inserted and lit a cigarette in his long holder; but today we were the only two people in an empty classroom until the teaching assistant appeared after a long wait. "There's no class today. . . . Where are you boys from?" We told him where we grew up. "Only a couple of fools from Bermuda and Georgia would have such little sense as to come out in a nor'easter like this." That experience seemed to bond Harold and me.*

*We studied together for our comprehensive exams (where the learned professor of the early church, Georges Florovsky, chaired my orals committee). After graduation Harold and I made a two month long hosteling and backpacking tour of Europe. While hiking through the Black Forest in Germany an ancient crone hobbled out of a hut and screamed, "Ein Schwarzermann . . . A black man . . . I saw one before when I was a little girl." Harold didn't speak German. I'd just passed my language requirement in German, but I told him only later what she'd said.*

*We seemed to run into a group from Texas everywhere, that always announced in a loud stage whisper, "They must be queers, a white man and a black man going around together like that." Harold thought it was funny. I was not amused. Even though Harold believed it was unnecessary, I compulsively always paid an extra fee for seat reservations on the train to accompany our Eurail passes, when we were traveling long distances. On the leg from southern Germany to Florence, Italy, the reservations paid off and gave us our revenge. The train was packed, and the Texas group wandered back and forth, up and down the corridor often peering into our compartment. At last they flung open the door. "Is this compartment occupied? There're only two of you. Couldn't you move somewhere else?"*

*"We reserved our seats here, but we'd be glad to share the compartment with you." We even offered to share our lunch with them when they had improvidently neglected to bring any food. After several refusals and hours of hunger, they accepted some of our sandwiches. I imagined 'heaping burning coals of fire' on my enemies' heads.*

*In the fall Harold took a position in Princeton, New Jersey, at the oldest African American Presbyterian Church in America, and I headed for North Carolina. He wrote me that he had been dating a nurse and had fallen in love with her. To my everlasting disgrace I wrote him a long letter detailing how marrying a white woman would create obstacles to his career and prevent their full acceptance and that of their children in both the black and the white communities. I couched my remarks as mere social commentary; but later, and perhaps subconsciously even then, I knew they emerged out of my own unresolved latent racism. The letter hurt Harold deeply. I apologized and attempted to make amends, but I was prevented from a face to face reconciliation.*

*Soon after his marriage Harold accepted a pastorate in Ohio. He had not lived there long before a terrible flood occurred, and Harold being Harold dived into the rushing water in an attempt to rescue two little girls and drowned. I wrote his widow about my grief and devoted affection, and she responded graciously telling me how often Harold had spoken of me and how much he had valued our friendship, but her words did little to assuage my shame.*

∽

*Although I had scholarships both as an undergraduate at Duke and as a seminarian at Harvard, I had to work during the school terms to supplement my income and pay my bills (this was the era of pay-as-you-go before student loans were common). The only position available during my freshman year at the Divinity School was as youth director at the Roslindale Congregational Church. It took a month for the teenagers to understand what I was saying in my Georgia drawl and for me to understand them with their South Boston brogue; but they soon became as fond of me as I was of them. They would appear at my dormitory room at all hours of the day and night, often at the most inconvenient and inappropriate times.*

*In order to keep my scholarship I had to maintain a B average. As my first set of semester exams approached I told them that they must not come to my dorm because I had to spend every moment studying. They seemed to understand how important it was for me to study; and they stayed away until the night before my most dreaded test, when they burst into my room, literally carried me down the stairs holding a cloth over my mouth, and kidnapped me. They put me in the back of one of their vintage, banged-up cars and took me to an amusement park and forced me onto a roller coaster. They told me that I had to get away from my books and loosen up and think about something else. I was and still am terrified of thrilling carnival rides.*

*The exam the next day produced my best grade for that semester. I learned that in times of stress and anxiety, I really do need to get away from my obsessions and find a way outside my fearful anticipations, but never, never again on a roller coaster.*

*My sophomore year of seminary I was offered the position of assistant chaplain to undergraduate Baptist students at Harvard and MIT. I gratefully and enthusiastically accepted the job, but the teenagers from Roslindale will always have a special place in my heart. When I graduated from the Divinity School, they appeared in my dorm room after a long absence and presented me with a beautiful leather briefcase, which I've always suspected may have been stolen but, however it was obtained, was no less appreciated and treasured.*

∾

*Although the practice of confessing one's sins in the presence of a priest is neither as greatly emphasized nor as frequently practiced among Episcopalians as it is among Roman Catholics, it is one of the great spiritual resources available in our branch of the Christian Church. It was my privilege to be involved as a priest in the sacramental rite of Reconciliation from time to time over the years, especially during the Lenten season, and has been my very great privilege occasionally to hear the confession of sin by people who were dying. Although hearing other people confess their sins offered me many insights into my own humanity, the solemn confidentiality implicit in that practice prevents much discussion of those moments even by way of summary. The one thing that startled me, however, was how trivial many of the issues confessed seemed. They often appeared to confirm the jokes and jibes of the more evangelical community about the practice of confession. Unlike the impression of popular fiction in which a dying confession exposes scandalous behavior and heinous crimes, what people said often seemed almost silly. I felt at times like blurting out, "Why are you wasting your dying breaths tell God about THAT?" Then I realized that our small betrayals are often most emblematic of our failure to be fully human. Even my own confessions of sin, both by myself and in the sacramental rite of Reconciliation, were often remembered objectively and in retro-*

*spect as perhaps trivial and silly, but they also epitomized my failure to be the man I knew that God had created me to be.*

*Conversely my fervent petitions expressed at length with tears and urgent emotion to God, which at the time seemed earth shattering, later came to be understood as unimportant and superficial. In my teens and early twenties I prayed to be popular, but the truth of the old cliché, 'be careful what you pray for, lest your receive it,' was understood later, when as a priest I could have wished for greater anonymity. If I had become a member of the young 'in crowd,' I could never have developed later insights into my own humanity and empathy with other people. Later I prayed no less earnestly that my fiction would become famous and successful, at least published and respected. To a great extent I'm still waiting for a more mature perspective on that, but I am convinced that God has my best interest in mind for not responding favorably to those pleas.*

∽

*Most functions of a priest's work overlap and replicate those of other professions. Religious counseling is not greatly different from secular counseling. Preaching and teaching follow the same practices of other teachers and orators. Conflict resolution between squabbling factions employs the same skills that arbitrators and negotiators and especially parents use—it's not surprising that we're often called "fathers." The onerous administration of a parish, which occupies more of our hours than any other task, would be familiar to any business executive. Perhaps our roles are distinguished mostly by having to do everything in a modern world of specialization; as a colleague observed, we may be last generalists.*

*One aspect of our work is unique, however—when we officiate in the sacraments, especially in celebrating the Eucharist. It is difficult to praise and adore God while leading a service for a large congregation. My mind was often preoccupied with what comes next, with maintaining the rhythm and pace of the liturgy, with coordinating the people and elements to achieve dramatic coherence; but at certain moments, especially before the altar at Grace Church in Mt. Meigs, Alabama, as the Sursum Corda leads into the Sanctus then the first words and phrases of the Prayer of Consecration, I have a sense of standing at the very gate of paradise, between earth and heaven, at the threshold of the chamber of the divine presence. In those moments I know more clearly than at any others who I am, what I was created to be and to do, what is the foundation of all truth and meaning.*

∾

*My limited funds didn't allow me to return home for Thanksgiving during any of my four years at Duke, and I usually spent those holidays with Aunt Alice in Raleigh. On the day before Thanksgiving during my freshman year I asked Aunt Alice if I could borrow "Don Pedro," her old Plymouth coupe, and drive downtown to do some Christmas shopping.*

*By the time I reached the center of the unfamiliar city it had begun to snow very heavily, and unable to see signs I turned down a one-way street the wrong way. A police car immediately stopped me, and I received a ticket. I was terrified that Aunt Alice would learn what I had done in her beloved Don Pedro. I appealed to the policeman, and he told me that I could go immediately to the traffic court which was then in session. The judge was compassionate after hearing my story and assessed me with a very modest fine.*

*My roommate from Rochester, New York, also couldn't go home for Thanksgiving. I was to meet him and his girl friend's family for lunch in a restaurant in downtown Raleigh. I rushed from the courthouse and arrived breathlessly to find Graham and Mrs. Belisoli\* and her daughter already seated. Mr. Belisoli, who was unable to join us, was a prominent member of the North Carolina legislature; but as lunch progressed Mrs. Belisoli effusively introduced Graham and me to various state officials and legislators as they paraded by our table. When I saw the judge from my court appearance come in and sit to Mrs. Belisoli's back, I had a sick foreboding of what would happen as soon as lunch was over, and it did. When she introduced Graham and me—two outstanding, brilliant young*

Duke students—to the judge, he replied archly, "Yes, indeed, I've already had the pleasure of meeting one of them in my court this morning."

The snow storm increased in intensity during the afternoon, and Graham was unable to catch a bus back to Durham, where he had been invited to have Thanksgiving dinner in the home of friends. Aunt Alice's apartment was too small to host two men—she had only one rollaway bed—and it was determined that Graham and I would stay in a guest room in one of the girls' dormitories at Meredith College where Jenny Hanyen,* one of Aunt Alice's closest friends and the home economics professor, was the housemother. Miss Hanyen locked us into the room around 9:00 p.m. and told us that she would return to unlock the door around 7:00 a.m. An open transom over the door provided just enough space for the Meredith students, who were also unable to go home for the holiday, to taunt us and throw their stockings and even a few bras and panties into the room. The following morning we met several of the Meredith students, but we were never able to match any of them with their undergarments.

*(Although I have a good recollection of their names, I cannot accurately spell the names of these people I met more than fifty years ago.)

෧෨

The American Episcopal Church of the Holy Spirit faced the rather elegant Avenue Victor Hugo in Nice, France; but prostitutes soliciting customers strolled on the Rue Macaroni that ran beside the church. The proximity of call girls to our sacred space brought both humorous and poignant moments. A teenaged member of our youth group often spent Sunday afternoon at our house because her mother did not return from her assignations in time to pick her up.

Sometimes one of the girls would come into the church during Sunday services and sit on a pew by a single American male tourist, whisper to him, and if rejected, move on to another one until she found one to leave with her or gave up her efforts. Sometimes it was difficult for me to focus on my sermon from watching them. One particularly obnoxious older prostitute owned an automobile and drove up and down the street *about ten miles an hour gently beeping her horn at men. When Bishop Browning first arrived, so I was told, he went over to her car, believing her to be in distress, to the great amusement of his congregation.*

*Almost every afternoon I walked down to the beach after lunch in shorts and a tee shirt; but because I often wore a clerical collar going back and forth between the American and English churches, most of the people in the neighborhood recognized me. I had just passed the door-way of one of the small hotels where the girls took their clients, when I felt two palms on my back and heard a female voice say, "Pou-pou!" I whirled around.*

*Her face and voice were suddenly aghast. "Mon Dieu, le prêtre!" (My God, the priest!)*

*I laughed and gave her a pat on her arm. I rather enjoyed being identified as a man before I was recognized as a priest, in the order of life that Grady Jarrard had encouraged in his sermon at my Baptist ordination, although I don't think he had this particular circumstance in mind.*

～

*Although I am loathe to admit that I'm a control freak, I do like to know what's being planned and thus I am ambivalent (at best) about being surprised; but my family has seemed to enjoy surprising me on my birthday over the years.*

*Many people in our hometown liked to cut their Christmas trees on our farm, and my father generously allowed almost anyone to cut a tree with the provision that one of our family members would accompany them so that they would not damage the woods.*

*Mrs. Kellogg was the mother of one of my best friends, and Charles and I would usually cut a tree and bring it back for her approval to where she waited for us at her car. The year of my sixteenth birthday (on December 14) we cut tree after tree after tree, beautiful pines, aromatic cedars, none of which she liked. Finally we brought back the scraggliest, most misshapen, lopsided tree from that part of the woods. "Oh, that's perfect! Just what I want." I thought Charles' mother had completely lost her mind. When we returned to our house and opened the door, my friends yelled, "Surprise! Happy birthday!" The Kelloggs took home one of the first trees we'd cut The rejections had all been timed to keep me occupied; and they were eventually parceled out to other friends in town, although the straggly tree was never claimed by anyone.*

*Alejandro Martínez, a Nicaraguan friend, had promised to get a tempisque table for me, whose shape resembles a huge maple leaf. My first birthday after our marriage happened to fall on a Sunday. I had become more and more disgusted with Alex, who made one ridiculous excuse after another for failing to find my table. When I came home after the Sunday service, the curtains were suspiciously drawn; and as I opened the door Alex and his wife Julia and Rilla yelled, "Surprise! Happy birthday!" And there in front of the sofa was the most beautiful tempisque table that I've ever seen, complete with coffee tree trunk legs. (It was one of only four pieces of furniture we brought back to the U.S.A. from Nicaragua and one of the things we refused to part with when we downsized for our retirement home.)*

*As my seventieth birthday approached we all agreed that any celebration would be deferred until my grandson Lennox recovered from two surgeries on his leg. A week before my birthday, between the two surgeries, we drove up to Durham for supper in order to baby-sit so that Lauren and Neill could attend a business meeting. Lauren told us to bring along some Sunday clothes so that she could make a grandparents' photograph for a Christmas poster for Lennox's school—"all the children are bringing photos of their grandparents, and we just don't have a good one of you." When we opened the door my brother and his wife from Georgia and my sister and her husband from Virginia and my niece and her husband from Charlotte and Lauren and Neill and Lennox yelled, "Surprise! Happy birthday!"*

*Maybe I do like to be in control and know what's going on; but mostly, I think, I don't like being fooled and am reluctant to admit I'm gullible and stupid. My momentary annoyance is soon displaced, however, by a heart filled with joy and love and gratitude.*

∼

*When the letter from my agent in New York arrived with word that the last publisher had passed on what I had believed was my best effort, for which I had held my highest hopes, with her, of success, I stretched out on my bed. My disappointment was too dry and bitter for tears. My despair left me too exhausted and weak for even tearless sobbing. Lauren climbed up beside me, unaware of the source of my sorrow and pain—"I'm sorry, Daddy"—and nestled against me. She stayed there silently for a long time until I picked myself up and picked her up and went into the den to play with her.*

*In my arms before she was one year old Arabella would feel my face with her fingertips, like a blind person learning the contours of a countenance. No other baby nor child nor adult has ever explored the features of my visage as carefully as she, as if seeking a deep understanding of who I am.*

*After raucous horse-playing late in the afternoon at the end of a full day of baby-sitting, a weary Lennox crawled up into my lap and put his arms around my neck and without any prompting or suggestion, to my great surprise said spontaneously, "I love you, Abu"' (what he calls me, the abbreviation of abuelo, Spanish for grandfather), and gave me a kiss on the cheek.*

*Before they can articulate it in words—perhaps better than after articulation is mastered—children can help us to recognize what is most important in life and tell us who we really are and understand us at the core of our being. They know, and we sometimes forget, that being able to give love and being able to receive love are at the center of what it means to be human.*

www.ingramcontent.com/pod-product-compliance
Lightning Source LLC
Chambersburg PA
CBHW032101080426
42733CB00006B/375